The Days of Mars

The Colors of Vaud
This January Tale
Visa for Avalon
The Coin of Carthage
The Heart to Artemis
Ruan
Gate to the Sea
Beowulf
Roman Wall
The Player's Boy
The Fourteenth of October

The DAYS of MARS

A Memoir, 1940-1946

By BRYHER

A Helen and Kurt Wolff Book
Harcourt Brace Jovanovich, Inc.
New York

ISBN 0-15-124055-8
Library of Congress Catalog Card Number: 79-174505
Printed in the United States of America

To
The Lowndes Group

Foreword

In wartime the only things that matter are a blanket, some food and one's friends. What I called the "Lowndes Group" had begun to form round H.D., before I arrived from Switzerland. Besides Hilda, her daughter Perdita and myself, there was Norman Pearson directly he arrived from America in April, 1943, the Sitwells, the Hendersons, the Dobsons, Robert Herring, George Plank, Mr. Baylis, Philip Frere and Mrs. Ash. Of course we had many other friends, mine being mostly in Cornwall, but we of the Group lived in or near London and shared our parcels, our rumors and our news, throughout the war.

What we should have done without Norman Pearson I do not know. Hilda had met him in New York but my friendship with him began only after he landed in England in 1943. He rescued Perdita from a dreary job in the country to do far more interesting work in London and, after its liberation, in Paris, and kept up our spirits during that final difficult year when we were too exhausted to care whether or not we survived until the peace.

Cole Henderson was an artist who had been a friend of Hilda's almost since she had arrived in England. I met Cole myself in 1920 and took her to see my mother, they subsequently became great friends. Her husband, Gerald, was librarian at St. Paul's and part of its famous Watch. He took me round Elizabethan London during some of the quieter Sunday afternoons and I owe him much gratitude for having made many dreary days less grim. He was severely injured during a raid and both of them died a few years after the war, largely as a result of its hardships.

I shall always be immensely grateful to Mrs. Ash, not only because she refused to let "those Nassis" keep her from coming up from Battersea every weekday to keep the apartment spotless in spite of the dust from the raids but for her comments on the Government and red tape. She was part of the very soul of England, afraid of nobody and able to expose the stupidity of certain people and regulations in pungent and most colorful speech.

Robert Herring had come to us on *Close Up* in 1927 and had afterwards become editor of *Life and Letters*

To-day in 1935. He had been rejected for medical reasons from military service and he carried on the magazine from different places throughout the whole of the war. It was an astounding feat because our different offices were always getting bombed, usually just as the paper was going to press.

The four Dobsons lived in Kent but came to see us whenever they could until their war service scattered them around the globe. Mervyn was in the army, Mary in the Wrens, Norah worked on a farm and Silvia who was a writer and therefore particularly linked to Hilda, eventually drove a truck round Italy on civilian rescue work. I have always been sorry that her vivid account of her experiences has never been published.

George Plank sacrificed his life to his principles. ("Dangerous things, principles!" Norman Douglas used to say.) He had been born in Pennsylvania and was known for his illustrations and cover designs, they appeared frequently in American and some English magazines, but he had settled in Sussex, built a red brick cottage there, designed by Lutyens, and naturalized as an Englishman. He joined the Home Guard in 1940 as soon as it was formed but he was too old for the heavy digging and the prolonged exercises in wet fields. He became ill towards the middle of the war and never fully recovered. The letters he wrote to me weekly gave me a wonderful picture of life in a village near a bombing run, and of the gradual ending of a traditional way of life. I have always regretted, as a historian, that a collection of them could not appear as a book.

Mr. Baylis worked for a firm that had done legal business for my father. He helped me to find my way through the intricacies of wartime red tape when I was required to sign every document or application form according to a long formula that ended "resident at Burier, Vaud, Switzerland, at present residing by Act of God at 49 Lowndes Square, London S.W.1, England." It seemed to be asking a lot of Heaven to be so interested in my changes of address.

It is always friendship that counts in the long dreary days that are full of hardships rather than valor.

The Days of Mars

1940

At midday on the 28th September, 1940, I reached H.D.'s apartment at 49 Lowndes Square, after a rough flight from Lisbon and a night at some seaside hotel. I have never discovered where the seaplane actually landed us although I think it may have been Poole. Hilda was out having lunch but she returned shortly after my arrival, less surprised to find me sitting on my suitcase than I was to be in London, and she remarked by way of greeting, "Osbert told me you would be coming over with the invasion barges. Did you?" Everything, as she opened the door, seemed very strange.

I arrived in a belligerent frame of mind and I did not have "a good war." I had had to leave my home, my dogs, my library and many friends; it seemed unlikely that I should see them again. What use was it to me now that I had known the war to be inevitable? "I warned you," I kept repeating, "why didn't you listen to me?" It made people angry and words could not bring back the things that I had lost. The five and a half years between my arrival in London and my return to Switzerland on the 5th of April, 1946, was a time of almost complete frustration, endurable only because I shared it with friends.

By the time I got to England, most Londoners were living in a state of bewilderment and guilt. "It's your own fault," I hastened to assure them, "you lost the Czech army in 1938 and the goodwill of the thousands who have since been liquidated and what did you do with the time you gained?" They were angry, they did not want to have their guilt confirmed (who does?) and they walked away murmuring their sacred slogan, "If only the leaders could have got together round a conference table" without the least realization that international promises seldom hold unless backed by force. Just what use were words against a ruthless enemy magnificently equipped? "Realize that human life does not matter to your antagonists," I insisted, "if you believe in freedom you must be prepared to defend it." I was more than unpopular, I was considered to be treacherous, although I cannot imagine why it was treachery to point out the truth.

4

The Government had had almost eighteen months (if the period of the "phony war" were taken into consideration) to prepare for battle but what had they done? They had neither imported foodstuffs in sufficient quantity, drawn up a proper and comprehensive rationing scheme such as we had in Switzerland nor pushed the construction of aircraft to the full. They had flung away much of the nation's foreign reserves in panic selling after the Fall of France. The measures that they were imposing about the time of my arrival were planned in haste, often wasteful and largely unfair.

I had lived for a year under the Swiss regulations. The authorities there had prepared their scheme scientifically and at leisure several years previously. Our blackout had been inspected before Munich, food control came into force on the outbreak of war and functioned perfectly. Quality was stressed rather than quantity and they had stockpiled immense reserves. It was said in England that we gave the children in England an adequate diet but that was propaganda. The ones I met were always hungry and their parents undernourished. Of course this is not the picture that was presented to the world but it comes from direct observation and was for me a depressing lesson; control the Press and other methods of influencing public opinion and a nation can be persuaded into believing whatever a government wishes. I often wonder today when I read about the rejection of order by the young if this is not due to memories inherited from parents who were adolescent during the war and suffered so much from austerity and restraint?

"Your rebellion goes back to the Forties," I think, as they stroll noisily down the streets in their dirty clothes, "it does not belong to the Sixties at all."

The English had no clear picture of invasion. Unfortunately for myself, I had, and I was anxious about my friends. I was never so afraid during the raids as I had been on that day in Switzerland when we had been warned to be ready to resist the German army, no doubt because I had seen what had happened to people whom the Nazis had tortured. I begged my cousin Hilda (H.D.), who was an American by birth, to rejoin her relatives there. I knew the war would hit her harder than it would hit us, she was so sensitive to noise, so thin and tall that it was obvious she was already suffering from the lack of protein in our diet. "Now?" she said, wrinkling up her Ionic nose (I have seen so many Greek statues that might have been portraits of her), "Now? Of course not."

So I walked across the park to the American Consulate in Grosvenor Square and handed back the immigration visa that had carried me across Portugal. "Don't you want to use it?" they politely inquired.

"If I did, would you want me as a citizen?" A particularly loud burst of gunfire shook the room at that moment and we all laughed. I believed that invalids and elderly people ought to leave if they had the opportunity but I was less sure about the children unless there were special circumstances. It is difficult for the young to fit into a community later on when they have missed a national experience. I might have considered going to New York myself in sheer disgust at the Munich muddle but I was not going to desert my friends.

The next step was to find a job. I was a trained observer of European politics, I had various *tuyaux* abroad that could have been most useful I was told when it was too late, I spoke French and German fluently and had brought a recommendation from the consul at Montreux. I should like to think that my warnings had so irritated the Establishment that they would have nothing to do with me but I suspect my work had never been noticed and that it was merely my long residence in Europe that was against me. Once, and once only, in the middle of the war, I was offered a job in Australia! By that time, life was extremely difficult and I saw no reason why I should leave my friends, they were all I had, to spend an indefinite period in an unknown land and I refused it. So seeing that a deeper than usual knowledge of the Continent had become a blind alley and that help was needed at *Life and Letters To-day,* a monthly magazine devoted to literature and edited by my friend, Robert Herring, where all but two of the staff were now in the army, I went back to familiar work. I had previously collected material for the paper from different countries in Europe but now as the editorial side had never been my métier, I answered letters and did odd jobs.

Life was strange and familiar at the same time, yet in spite of the bombing I found the Second War so much easier to bear than the First. We were all "in it" and there was not the dreadful gap between soldiers and civilians that had caused so much stress in 1914.

There were even a few links during the first month between Switzerland and England. The porter stopped me as I was going out, a couple of days after my arrival. "They say you have come over from Montreux, madam, what's the town like now?"

I was a little surprised at his interest. Vaud seemed far away but it had always been a favorite place with tourists. "Oh, it's much as usual except that the roads are empty. Only cars needed for essential work get petrol."

"Has the market place changed?"

"No, they still sell vegetables there, they are not rationed."

"It looked so beautiful. Of course, I only saw it upside down."

I believe the correct expression is "stunned with surprise" and I can think of no better words to express my feelings. "Upside down?"

"I was an acrobat." No poet ever spoke more proudly. "We played all the towns along the coast." He knew his lake, we always spoke of it locally as "the coast." He grasped my hand and shook it as it had never been shaken before, not even when I was young by my fencing master. It was as if some iron instrument of torture from the Middle Ages had gripped it. "I'm English, of course, but I was born at Geneva in a tent."

I have always been sorry that I did not stop to ask him more about his experiences but I was still bewildered by my journey and in a hurry to collect my identity card and ration book. Before I could find him again, he had gone to a more important job than guarding our doors. Yet I often wonder what happened to him when I walk now beside the market place on a summer day when they are putting up the side shows for some fête. The dusty ground looks so hard, the gables so dangerous, and how do the swans and the shouting, excited children appear to a man swinging head downwards from a rope? It is a corner of Montreux that has scarcely changed since I was ten. There are tall new buildings to the left and right of it but the steamer comes into the landing place, the stalls are crowded on a market day, and there are still round-abouts and peddlers at the summer fair.

The acrobat was not my only contact with home. I had to buy something at a neighboring store after a night of particularly noisy raids and happened to mention that I had just got back to England. "Montreux! You come from Montreux," the assistant said, "aren't you lucky? I went there on my honeymoon and last night when a bomb came down in the next street, I clutched Hubby and said, 'If we've got to die, let's remember that balcony where we stood and looked at the lake with all the stars shining above our heads.' "

Switzerland was a bright ribbon across their otherwise drab lives, and these strangers were full of sympathy. It was otherwise with my friends; for some reason that I do not understand even today, they would not allow me to speak about my home. Osbert Sitwell apart, they did not even want to know how I had reached London although it had been rather more than an adventurous journey. I did not want commiseration but the barrier puzzled me. I had spent five summers in the Alps as a child and I had lived afterwards for eighteen years in Vaud. The day that we were threatened with invasion it became a part of me. I have three countries, England, Switzerland and America and I am proud of them all. I had come to London simply because at a time of adversity and danger, I wanted to be with my friends.

I remembered a bit of advice from the First World War. Never register all the members of a household at the same shop. One part of Lowndes Square was in Westminster but our side was in Chelsea so as soon as I got my ration book I took it not to Hilda's grocer but to a large neighboring store. It was there that I met Susy, a few days after my arrival. She was standing behind the bread counter with tears literally streaming down her cheeks. There had not been any raid the previous night or news of any battle but I muttered a word of sympathy. "Oh, madam, it's this wartime bread, mee plate stuck in it and it broke."

"Dear me, how very unfortunate."

"Yes, madam, it means a day's pay getting the fitting and the new set will cost me more than my Christmas bonus. You see, madam, us business girls have got to have our teeth."

The bread, though unrationed, was appalling. Again I wished (oh, how often I was to wish) that the Swiss could have organized our food system. Our loaves in Vaud had been limited in quantity but excellent. Help was essential for Susy so, cursing the Establishment, I hurriedly pressed on her a little financial aid. I got a dazzling smile from her a few days later and we were firm friends until she died, shortly after the war. She would probably have lived to a good age if it had not been for its hardships.

Susy was my first new friend but I had soon had others, in "veg," in "groceries" and "pots and pans." I knew how they had to get up at five thirty of a cold winter morning to make their beds and get a cup of tea before hurrying to a windy corner to get one of the crowded, infrequent buses to their work. I heard what they did on Sundays (mostly they slept), their scruples about their rose bushes, ought they to scrap them and plant lettuces instead, where they would go the next Bank Holiday afternoon. All they asked in return was a comfort I could not give them, some assurance that this time it would not be a "long war." Occasionally I could find them an oddment for which they had no time to search. Once one of them pressed a tiny packet of custard powder into my hand. "She offered me five shillings for it" ("she" was a woman disappearing into the next department) "but I kept it for you, dear, you really care about my aunt's rheumatic knee." And it was true. I cared, profoundly cared about a poor old woman hit by this second war through the stupidity of our politicians and thus deprived of the legitimate small comforts due to her age. I was not myself a custard addict but it was an accolade.

My great friends, however, lived in the neighboring

11

street. Hilda had discovered the *Warming Pan* some years earlier and usually went there for lunch. Up to 1941, its owners, Selina and Angelina, supplied their clients with soup, meat, two veg and dessert for two shillings and ninepence. They were country people, they bought all the ingredients they could directly from farms and the cooking was plain but excellent. Such places are now extinct. I liked it because, as I said, I could go there without fear. There was a large notice, *Dogs Welcome*, hanging on the door and as I am to those, but only those, who know me intimately, Fido, I felt at ease and knew that I should not be hustled out to eat from my bowl somewhere under the stairs. Up to the time that the restaurant was badly damaged by a bomb, Selina saw that our food was as honest as possible and not composed completely from powders.

My dear, dear Selina. She was a symbol to me of the essential soul of England. She did not encourage casual conversation when we went up to her desk to pay our bills but if I were careful, I could manage to exchange a few words with her. She and her partner had built their business up from scratch and now, just as they were beginning to pay off the debts that had always been a nightmare to them, most of their customers had gone into the country or joined the Women's Services. It is always the middle groups that suffer most in war and the Victorian doctrine that hard work is its own reward flops at once in a time of national disaster.

The raids were heavy throughout October. I went out gloomily one morning with my basket to get our rations and saw a huge crater at the end of Basil Street. Somebody had fetched a large plaster bulldog, I assume from Harrods because they were then on sale there, and stuck it on guard beside the biggest pile of rubble. At that moment *Beowulf*, my war novel, was conceived.

Many years later I tried to get one of the small plaster dogs to serve as a model for the book's jacket. The assistant, a look of horror on his face, assured me that they had never stocked anything so vulgar. "There wouldn't be any demand for it," he said, "I've never been asked for one."

"Of course not," I could not resist replying, "it was merely a national emblem."

Knowing the circumstances, I could forgive the man his shock but those plaster bulldogs were standing proudly about the streets in 1940. I saw another one in the Edgware Road.

Hilda had taken a small apartment in Lowndes Square some years previously at an annual rent of two hundred and fifty pounds. It is a measure of the present depreciation of money that when I last heard about it some years ago, it was said to be six hundred a year and there was a rumor subsequently that even this had been increased. She had a bedroom, a sitting room with a clear view across to Basil Street because the big block that now occupies what was then a vacant site was not built till after the war, a tiny bathroom, an equally small kitchen and a spare bedroom that she gave over to me. In addition, she had the use of a room for storage purposes in the basement. We slept there for a few nights at the beginning of the Blitz but soon gave it up because as Hilda sensibly remarked, "If we are going to be killed, let us be comfortable up to the last moment."

There was no room for a table in my room but there was a broad window ledge that I could use as a desk during the day; only at night because of the blackout, I had to sit on my bed and balance the typewriter on my knees. It got rather noisy one October evening but I had started on notes for *Beowulf* when there was a thundering knock and the superintendent burst in (he had a master key) with what appeared to be a revolver sticking out of his pocket. The blackout was in order, the curtains were drawn, there was not a crack of light showing anywhere. "That noise," he looked at me accusingly, "that cracking noise?"

"Is it the new weapon?" They had been warning us that the Germans were preparing a surprise and I had been discussing what it could be over supper with Hilda that evening.

"No, it was in here." He looked round and noticed my machine.

"You were *typing*."

I nodded.

"Never do that again in a raid. I thought you were signaling." He slammed the door as he left and I reflected dismally that the way of the artist is hard in war. It is not difficult to write during a Blitz, there is nothing else to do, but merely uncomfortable.

The English refused to publish *Beowulf*. They do not

14

want to remember. It was a documentary, not a novel, but an almost literal description of what I saw and heard during my first six months in London. It sold steadily if not brilliantly after the war in America. I loved my characters, especially Rashleigh, Ruby and Selina. Of course, I altered a few details of their lives but it was otherwise as authentic a record as I could make it.

I never actually met Rashleigh (that was not his real name) but we had corresponded for years and as he earned his living painting miniatures on ivory of the *Victory*, what else could I call him but Horatio? He knew his boats. "I went in my youth to Australia in a sailing ship and learned all about square-rigged vessels." His wife, to whom he had been devoted, had recently died as well as a cousin, "now, alas, no more, save his delightful memory," his daughters were away nursing, his savings had practically disappeared. It would be hard to say which frightened him most, the war or modern painting. Yet I could feel from his letters a complete dedication to art although due to early influences or perhaps the lack of funds to study either in London or abroad he had never progressed beyond neat landscapes seen through Victorian eyes or studies of red sails and coasters in a storm. People complained that he was a conventional figure when they read *Beowulf*. He was, but I did not invent him, I knew him. If we had met, I should have shocked him profoundly. Yet the only law in art is never to despise the seeker and I wrote to him regularly to inquire what was happening to the seascape he was painting and how he was managing on his rations? I like to think that my letters helped him a little till he caught a chill in an air-raid shelter during some heavy raids on the South Coast. The illness turned to pneumonia and, mercifully, he died.

I, also, have laughed at such people and I have always wanted "the art after tomorrow" but fate gives all of us a different apprenticeship to serve and at the end it is the use we make of it that matters, not our successes.

"London can take it" was not a slogan, it was a statement of fact. The bombing that October seemed continuous. Some people pretended that it was not happening at all, others endured hours of uncomfortable travel daily in order to spend the night in the supposedly safer countryside. The majority of us, however, "got on with it." People were not robots, they were afraid, but they expressed their feelings obliquely if at all. Still, I shall never forget a neighbor I met in the hall, he was evidently on his way to some function since he was carrying a gray top hat that I had not seen since Edwardian times. "I do hope we are not going to be disturbed by the guns all evening," he remarked as we braced ourselves against the wall when an explosion shook the neighboring street. I bowed as politely as circumstances permitted and murmured "Yes," knowing that he must be under a great emotional strain to have spoken to me. We had never been properly introduced.

The traditions held, if perhaps for the last time. A day or so later, I went into a grocer's shop in search of some small, as yet unrationed article. The alert had sounded but I had not bothered about it. Suddenly the floor heaved up, the assistant and I rolled to the ground as inextricably intertangled as a brace of lobsters, while the dust of ages enveloped us from the ceiling. "And the next thing, madam?" the grocer inquired as, shaking ourselves, we rose to our feet.

Some scenes defy words and one of these was the Underground. A few days after reaching London I went to visit friends at Edgware and coming back about six, saw one of the strangest spectacles that London can have witnessed during its long history, the camps along the platforms of the Tube stations. Not all things in wartime were bad. One of the taboos that the Blitz was breaking down was that it was wrong to speak to strangers. It is a mistake to suppose that it is the upper groups in a community that are aloof. I have always found that the top and the bottom of the ladder talk freely. The "professionally lonely" come from the lower middles who consider it to be a status necessity "to keep themselves to themselves." Many of these barriers broke with the raids. Cook, secretary, shopkeeper and workman sat on their rugs and sleeping bags, carefully arranged above a layer of old newspapers (I was assured that the *Times* was the thickest and most comfortable) leaving a few inches free here and there so that passengers alighting from the trains could struggle to the dangerous upper levels while they themselves smoked, drank tea, munched sandwiches and told each other stories. They were having, a number assured me, "the time of their lives." It was said that one lady slept under an eiderdown covered with blue silk but I did not actually see this myself. There were bundles of valuables that served as pillows, the occasional clock, much passing round of cigarettes. It combined the slight trepidation of a mixed group of holiday adventurers about to start on their first climb and the pseudo-resignation of the parlor maid, waiting for a chance to contradict the cook. Old men in second-hand clothes were in one ring, ladies saving their best furs in the more favored positions nearer the wall where there was less dust. A few people could not stand the noise and returned to their own beds but these shelters must have fulfilled a need beyond that of safety (was it perhaps for adventure?) because a couple of years later at almost the quietest moment of London's war, there were bunks lined with gay, chintz curtains the length of the platforms and officials spoke with pride about the "loyal few" who still spent their nights beside the clanging trains. In 1940, the scene was unforgettable. It was a science fiction novel in action although at the time I did not recognize it, not having then discovered the genre.

I sometimes wonder whether I should have survived the war if it had not been for Osbert's friendship and Edith's love. Sacheverell Sitwell was serving in the navy and for that reason I met him only much later. They had invited Robert Herring to stay with them in Derbyshire until he could find fresh quarters as both his house in Chelsea and the office of *Life and Letters To-day* had been badly damaged by bombs. Soon after my arrival I was asked to spend the following weekend with them.

I felt really stupefied with astonishment when I found I could buy a ticket and board a train without producing my passport or stating the purpose of my journey. People were talking calmly to each other about the bombing when I sat down in the railway carriage but I could not help thinking how little they knew about war. They had not seen the French soldiers with the soles looped to their boots by bits of string nor waited in desperate fear at a frontier post. I could forgive the "little people" for not understanding the real motives behind Munich but not these middle-aged men, chattering over their newspapers in apparent surprise. They ought to have known better. They had let things slide, murmuring, "Oh, it will settle itself somehow, there's too much at stake for the Germans really to go to war." Hoping for the best and doing nothing to achieve it is possibly the deadliest sin there is. How many millions died in Europe because the supposedly solid citizens of a dozen countries thought only of their village interests and never of the world?

The damp, October landscape I watched from the window took me right back to childhood. I saw myself, as if I were still there, sitting on a hassock in the nursery with a picture book on my knees. Two children on rough, brown ponies were galloping across a field of just the same green grass, with a few bramble hedges and a few red leaves at the side which we were passing now in the train. For a second, I wondered why I should recall so vividly a moment that had happened to me forty years earlier? Yet it was the far past that was a poster-colored reality, the present was a fog. I was only going to be away for two nights yet I already felt the shame that many of us noticed if we were outside London during the raids.

I missed a taxi at the station, that Osbert had sent to meet me because it had not occurred to me that taxis were still available. I walked up to Renishaw wondering where it was and what it was like. To say that I was amazed when I saw it would be an understatement. I had only thought about Osbert and Edith as fellow writers, we had never talked about homes. It was true that I had seen some of Osbert's treasures in his house in Chelsea when I had lunched with him there before the war but all I knew about Derbyshire was the address. The range of windows reminded me of those old Italian palaces that are a town in themselves and the formal garden was still a blaze of summer flowers. It was the first and last time that I saw it in its glory because by my next visit the beds were full of cabbages. The butler seemed a little startled that I was carrying my suitcase when he opened the door.

The dining room was full; besides visitors who were staying at Renishaw, people had come over from Sheffield, the nearest big town. I had expected to sit beside Robert Herring because although we had telephoned I had not seen him since landing. Instead I was put next to Charles Morgan and realized afterwards that it was yet another of Osbert's thoughtful acts. Morgan had many friends in France and was desperate for news. It was a relief to be questioned by somebody who knew the Continent and had also prophesied war from early in the Thirties. I was also glad to be able to talk about the problems of friends without meeting the resentment that so many had shown me in London. They said I had dodged their tribulations by remaining in Vaud for a year.

Sometimes one meets a person casually and recognizes a relationship due to a mutual admiration for some particular period or place. Neither of us could help our friends, we did not even know where they were. Had they left Paris, were they trapped in some corner of a remote province or already in prison? The deserted roads, the abandoned cars still lying in the ditches that I had seen during my journey, had almost annihilated hope. Almost, not quite; after a drive of sixteen hours during which time we had hardly seen one peasant in the fields, the coach in which we were traveling had drawn up in darkness in front of a little hotel somewhere in a city. I asked the name of the town and they answered "Cette." So I had Valéry's name and the memory of his poems to sustain me during the last night I was to spend on French soil for seven years.

I cannot remember our conversation word for word but Charles Morgan was even more pessimistic than I was about the length of the war and its effect upon civilization. We both knew how much had already been destroyed. I kept thinking of Sylvia Beach and Adrienne Monnier in Paris until it was almost as if they were waiting in another room. Europe, we agreed, if it emerged would be a different world. The young would not know what they had lost, the old would be too exhausted to care. A great civilization had been swept away in less than a fortnight and, as I was to observe later, little was salvaged. Paris in the Fifties was never the Paris of even the Thirties.

We started sentences to encourage each other, they broke off in the middle, we had no facts. All we could do was to sit side by side, a couple of shipwrecked sailors, still dazed by our own rescue and drawn together by a common anxiety about our friends. We never met again.

It was during this visit to Renishaw that my friendship with Edith began. I had met her a few times, always in the midst of a crowded tea party, in the apartment where she had lived for a time in Bayswater. Now, and Edith herself could not have realized how much it meant to me, once the visitors had left she read me poems, sitting outside on the terrace in the pale, October sunshine. It was indescribably peaceful to sit listening to the poems with the sweep of the garden in front of us and the feeling that beyond the poetry there could be something indestructible in the mind. Even now, more than twenty years after the so-called peace, Renishaw is a circlet of golden moments uncovered from a temple's dust.

My own past caught me up. I walked across the edge of a forlorn Hyde Park full of guns and searchlights, to seek consolation in a bookshop. There, turning over the pages of a just-published volume, Koestler's *Scum of the Earth*, I saw the name Walter Benjamin and read of his death on the Spanish frontier. I had believed him to be safe.

The previous April, Sylvia and Adrienne had taken

me to meet him at a café near the rue de l'Odéon. He had seemed so much a part of Paris, of that blue, smoky atmosphere where everyone was sipping bitter coffee and arguing about metaphysics. The scholar is truly afraid that action, even if it is harmless, may disturb his contemplation and Adrienne had begun a dialogue with him that evening that had carried them on a chase of some philosophical comet where neither Sylvia nor I could follow them. An artist thinks in a different way, linking present impression to past experience. Suddenly Benjamin had asked us if we thought that he could live in New York? What could we say? Other than Paris, there were few places where he would have felt at home.

I tried to temporize, always a form of cowardice, but after we left, Adrienne asked me whether as Benjamin had received an American visa, he ought to leave at once? As regards my own refugees, I had always told them to go if possible the day they received their papers. This time I trusted to emotion rather than reason and agreed with her she should wait before urging him to leave, to see how things turned out. What would he do, we wondered, in a small bedroom in windswept New York where there were no cafés at that time and few friends? I had heard while still in Switzerland that he had got away from Paris in time, we had tried to send him funds for the further journey to Lisbon but it is possible they never reached him; we supposed that he had landed safely in America. Now I read in a bookshop the bare fact of his death. There was an air raid in progress, guns were thundering in the distance but all I could feel was how lucky we were to be part of a nation fighting back with every weapon it possessed. Yet what did my fellow citizens know of the terror of being chased and tortured for supposed crimes of which the victims had never even heard? Why did the religious institutions of Europe fail to denounce the Nazis early in the Thirties? Some clergymen, in particular from some Protestant sects and above all, the Quakers, were heroic in their efforts to rescue the victims but in general the established churches looked the other way. A condemnation by them might have saved thousands of lives and would have given a lead to citizens to accept more refugees into their homes.

The full story of Benjamin's death reached us only after the war.

London grew grayer and dingier. We wondered if the dust could have come from the Great Fire in 1666. Yet I can truthfully say that I was not afraid during the first raids. I had been inoculated against what I called "this simple terror" by my experience abroad. Yet I had been unable to make the English understand. Whenever I had told them what was happening in Europe, all they replied was, "Very sad, dear, but if I were you, I would not get mixed up in these foreign disputes." Now they were getting their answer. In bombs. I myself declared war on the Establishment. Had they not brought us to this sorry pass because unlike the "Old Contemptibles" they had been afraid of Germany? Around me the deluded but by now awakened populace was amazingly, fantastically heroic. "We shall never see the Nazis marching through London," my neighbors declared in the queue although apart from a few Spitfires, I could see nothing myself to prevent them, and these same Spitfires, I was told, had only been developed at the beginning through private enterprise and not with Government aid. I had warned people since 1932, nobody had listened to me so I decided that my moral duty was to grumble. I was reasonably cheerful if uncertain whether we could survive the winter, invasion seemed probable and we did not even have enough weapons to arm the Home Guard. "By Pike and Mace, or With Bulldog to Victory," I wrote to a friend in America; "my chief preoccupation is, if we are to act as powder monkeys in the Blitz, must we wear pigtails? As for myself, it is sheer stupidity to go on breathing and I heard that slogan about 'Building a Better Britain' in 1918. Oh, if dinosaurs had been fluid and more adaptable, there need never have been a human race."

Still there was one consolation, it was Cochrane. The schools are careful never to mention him because he is all that they dislike, a rebel who laughed at the Establishment and was successful in carrying out his plans of which they disapproved. In 1809 a large French fleet was assembled in the Aix Roads for a probable invasion of England. Cochrane prepared a plan to destroy these vessels that would have shortened the war by several years and saved thousands of lives. The Admiralty rejected it but eventually gave him a grudging permission to make a sortie with four small fire boats. With them, inadequate as they were, he destroyed six French battleships. He could have won a complete victory but the Admiralty refused to let the rest of the English fleet move until it was too late. I had often thought about it during the Thirties as the classic example of what was still happening in official England and now whenever I was asked to fill up in triplicate a particularly idiotic form, I would shake my head, remind the functionaries that we were supposed to conserve paper and mutter as I signed it, "Remember the Aix Roads."

The official argument against Cochrane is that he was said to have swindled people on the Stock Exchange through having a false rumor spread that the French were asking for peace. He denied the charge and it seems unlikely he would risk his career knowingly in such a way. If he were responsible, as a few believe, it was surely due to the exasperation that he must have felt with official circles round him. He was dismissed from the fleet but England's loss was South America's gain. Chile, Peru and Brazil won their independence from Spain largely through his efforts and up to a few years ago, remembered his anniversary. He helped the Greeks in their war of independence and was eventually restored to his full honors in England. Marryat was one of his officers and you can read about Cochrane in *The King's Own*.

Cochrane and Sir Richard Burton have been two of the Englishmen I have admired the most, far more than the "official" heroes. Both spent their lives fighting the Establishment and both helped to establish a freer world.

The rationing system in England was absurd. "Bread is unrationed," the bureaucrats said proudly but it was not even sawdust; we wondered what it could contain and we knew it was unrationed because it was uneatable. It turned a particularly livid hue of green within a few hours and was so hard that the populace referred to it as "our secret weapon." I hated Authority less because it made rules than because it was stupid and therefore I prepared a little talisman to hand round so as to remind Londoners of their responsibilities.

> I wonder what would have happened to Drake
> when they asked him the Spaniards to slaughter
> had he fed on a diet of parsnip and hake
> and a glass of pure water?
>
> We look at the skies and think Nelson was fine,
> his speeches and manner we parrot,
> But would he have battered those ships of the line
> on a chew of raw carrot?
>
> We shiver on roofs between blackout and dawn,
> while Whitehall (hush hush) studies Plato.
> But I wonder politely just why we were born
> to be gay and shout hey
> and hurray for the Government Food Control
> on the half of a frigid potato?

Some seemed uneasy as I pressed it into their hands, others got the message.

The dust and smell of the raids were far removed from the snowy mountain crests above the placid lake at Burier and, besides, I missed the country. I feel more at home as a rule in it than in a town. It was George Plank who eased these first transitional months by inviting Hilda and myself for weekends in the Sussex cottage that Lutyens had designed for him. At first we went together but as the months went on and the journey got more difficult, I usually went alone.

George, like Hilda, came originally from Pennsylvania. An orphan, brought up by relatives, he had suffered from a narrow and much restricted childhood. Later he had gone to art classes after working at a monotonous and unrewarding job all day. People suddenly became interested in his drawings and he began to sell his work to a lot of well-established magazines. He had come to London originally on a visit but was so happy in England that he decided to settle in Sussex although he went back to New York every other year to keep in contact with the art world there and to visit his sisters. Like myself, he had realized that war was inevitable by the middle of the Thirties, but instead of crossing the Atlantic, he immediately applied for British citizenship. It was granted to him about 1938. He joined the Home Guard directly it was formed but this act was probably responsible for a severe illness towards the middle of the war. He was too old, too slightly built, to stand the constant exposure and the heavy digging of trenches that we all suspected would be of little use if there were an invasion. I have often felt

28

since how little gratitude we showed to the many Americans who deliberately chose to share our hardships and dangers. They were "Loyalists" the other way round.

It was a refuge, not precisely because it was safe, we were probably below a bombing run and often heard the German planes overhead, but because with our prewar records of the awareness of danger, we could now ignore events and talk about art or what we called "real life," meaning the search for truth, why there were so few exact words for color, if I should get to Cornwall again or whether Hilda would stop writing on account of the noise? I did not often go to Sussex after 1940 because of increasing work elsewhere but George came to see Hilda and myself occasionally at Lowndes and we kept in contact through our weekly letters. Later on, he was able to visit us after our return to Switzerland and I always tried to see him whenever I was in London. He died in 1965.

1941

1941 was the worst year of the war for me in many ways. I was still linked to Burier where I had lived for so many years and I had not yet found a corner for myself in England. Besides, although I had thought of doing a lot of things in my life, I had never imagined myself climbing up the Sheffield streets in a woolly coat and heavy boots, desperately clutching a pole striped, peppermint fashion, in red and green, with *Nord Kap* in large letters round the top. I caught sight of myself in a mirror standing in an isolated, undamaged shop and thought "How odd! How very odd!" Yet nobody noticed us although Robert Herring who had produced the poles, wore Eskimo boots laced up to the knees. He had found that it would be months before his house in Chelsea could be repaired and the office of *Life and Letters To-day* had also been hit, fortunately at night when nobody was inside, so he had rented a house temporarily at Eckington and was editing the magazine from there. His account of the bombing of London in the November issue of the magazine is one of the most accurate and vivid descriptions of the raids that I have read. The office boys had been called up; our secretary Miss Voules and I were trying to cope in London with those matters that did not need to be referred to the editor but from time to time one of us had to go north for a weekend that combined a brief change with business consultation.

A century's dust was mixed with the snow and the curious smell that bombing always left. Getting up the steep hill was a nightmare, the water from the hoses used against the fires had frozen into a lake and the dark lines of grimy paving stones under the ice gave us the feeling that we were walking over tombs. As Robert had predicted, we needed our poles to keep upright far more now than on that distant day when we had climbed up the North Cape. "I don't feel like a Lapp" was all I had the strength to moan as we came to the shell of a great building where thin, entirely black icicles dangled in a menacing way from shattered blocks of masonry, and I remembered grim accounts of how people had been killed by the snapping of such icicles in the mountains. Below, in what had been the cellars, the bottom was full of a gray, grimy powder that had frozen into wavy ridges. It was something we saw but that our senses could not believe. Here and there a shop that had escaped was doing "business as usual" among the ruins and we had come precisely in search of office supplies because much of the magazine's stationery had been destroyed in the London raid.

"It's important to keep *Life and Letters* going," Robert said.

It was. Throughout the war we sold every copy that we had enough paper to print, but on that morning in Sheffield I cannot say that I cared why it had happened. These periods of numbness were frequent at the beginning of the war, later they turned to disillusionment and rage. Yet I have found few studies of the reaction of the populace. Why were we braver at some moments than at others, why could a comparatively light raid cause more panic than a more severe one and rumors be, as a rule, more potent than facts? There was relatively little aggression yet sometimes an intense feeling of guilt that the crowd could not explain and to the end of the war many people did not understand why it had happened. The one thing that united us was disbelief in any form of official pronouncement. It is too late now for any such inquiry, people would "arrange" their memories and feelings, but it seems to me a tragedy that a psychological investigation in view of future defence, was not carried out by independent observers at the time.

It is difficult to understand the general boycott of *Life and Letters To-day* by present literary historians of the period. Besides contributions from the Sitwells, H.D., Elizabeth Bowen, Dylan Thomas, Vernon Watkins, Alex Comfort and many other writers, we printed, I believe, the first story by Sartre to be translated into English and an early tale by Kafka. Adrienne Monnier sent us material by Henri Michaux and other French writers and until the post ceased in 1940, we always stressed our connection with France. I sometimes wonder whether it was because we were able to cover our expenses without a subsidy after the first few issues? Did this cause the paper to lose in esteem? It is an interesting psychological point.

So we struggled up the icy streets in search of envelopes and though I was not allowed to speak about Switzerland, I thought of it.

We are what our childhood makes us. Long before I heard of Freud I was interested in reading accounts of first memories and impressions. My own experience had taught me that the roots of life were there but it was never certain, and that was the adventure, how they would emerge. It was partly because of this belief and partly because of a poem with that title by Robert Browning that I called my first book *Development*. The two volumes I now discovered were linked to this interest and not only gave me great pleasure but won me lasting friendships. They were *A London Child of the Seventies* (and its sequels) by Molly V. Hughes and *Within the City Wall* by Margaret Phillips.

If I enjoy a book I often write to its author. It seems to

me a matter of politeness between one artist and another. So having read *A London Child* I wrote to Molly at once. I had been born thirty years later but the Victorians disliked change and our memories touched at many points. I had also had the "box of plain bricks," some of the books and the wooden horse and cart. I remembered the gas brackets being lit at night and the drives in a hansom cab when the horse looked so powerful and the ground so far away. Like Molly, I had picked primroses and looked for hazelnuts, walking miles across the fields in double the clothes that would be considered necessary now. Besides, she was half-Cornish and Cornwall was my own, if adopted, part of England.

We began to exchange letters and then came a February day when Molly had to come up from Cuffley where she lived to do some errands in London and we met. I think it must have been at the Underground because I remember walking with her along the Brompton Road. She was short, wiry and with such merry eyes. It is often a little difficult to break the ice on such occasions because the correct beginning of "I like your book so much" is very formal and it would be more enthusiastic to say slangily, "Something in it hit me" which is a far more precise description of what actually happens. With Molly, however, there was no need to say anything at all. We started towards Lowndes Square which she considered too fashionable an address until I assured her that my cousin had taken her apartment before the roof was on the building and told her the rent. She went on chattering gaily until she paused, looked at me seriously and asked me a question about a scholarly book much in the news at that moment but which I had not read. I seldom pretend to knowledge of a subject I have not studied; memory is limited although it may be large and the important thing is not to overload it but to know where to look up a fact and verify it. So I confessed my ignorance. Molly clutched my arm in relief, smiling her all-embracing smile, "Oh, I see you are truthful." It was a symbol of acceptance between teacher and new pupil and then she added, "Truth is the most important thing in the world."

I knew the code and how ruthlessly Molly would follow it; it was a counterpoise to the hypocrisy of her age. I was glad that I had passed her test but for myself truth is a two-edged weapon that needs to be wisely used. It may be as important to forget as to remember and often morality itself demands less bluntness and more understanding. Even though I saw Queen Victoria driving past me in the park where I was making mud pies, I suppose I am an Edwardian in point of age. Yet chronology has no hard borders and that earlier world survived around me in patches all the time that I was growing up and it impeded most of my ambitions. I have always been a feminist if that word means fighting for women's rights, and I glory in it. The bombs in both wars made no distinction as to sex and if the women had cracked up either time, our history would have been very different. Equality means equality, with no special privileges or advantages on either side but why should men have all the interesting jobs? I doubt if this present time offers as much freedom as we had in the Twenties; there was more liberty then, and a chance for development.

Once I had passed Molly's test everything was easy. To talk to her was to go back to the depths of memory and I understood her rather as the child who has been born in India can see the country through a language of familiar impressions if it is revisited in later years. Yet she got on more easily with Hilda than she did with me, she had once visited America for some educational congress, and they both had a love for exploring old churches. Hilda was more spontaneous and it often worked that way if I brought in new friends. I did the discovering, the "sniffing out" as I called it, but it was Hilda with her warmth and liveliness that consolidated the friendship. I am apt to look at people, wonder about them and be silent. It is due to a deep curiosity, I am afraid, not shyness.

Molly had brought us a loaf of her home-baked bread and I have never tasted better. Later I went to Cuffley for the day and saw the home about which she had written so much in her later books. It was full of warmth and gaiety, one could not be long in Molly's company without a laugh. We wrote each other frequent letters for years, she signed them "with love from a fellow rebel," and she allowed me to read some of her unpublished work. Alas, her neighborhood changed after the war, she was nearly blind and became too old to be left alone in the house she loved so much. Yet it is difficult to transplant the aged and she faded away in a strange environment and what was to her a totally alien age. We belong to our time and the most we can achieve as a rule is to be a generation ahead of it; if we tear up our roots how many can exist merely on air? Yet if people want to know what life was like for a poor scholar in one of the most opulent centuries England has known, they cannot do better than to study Molly's books. They are a record of an almost hopeless fight against prejudice when there was little chance for a woman, however brilliant her intellect, to get even a reasonably paid job. Today people find the Victorian age picturesque and amusing without understanding its cruelty. If they want a true photograph of part of it, they should consider what Molly had recorded.

Late in March Robert wrote and asked me if I would go to see Kenneth Maggs, the antiquarian bookseller in Berkeley Square, about some volume on Lapland. I do not think I had been in such a place before because books are my tools and I need modern editions for often rough use. While I was waiting for Mr. Maggs to get the information, I saw a small book bound in leather on the table in front of me and opened it out of curiosity. To my surprise, there was a picture inside it of two Elizabethans. I glanced at the title and saw the word *Philaster*. It took me back to my first discovery of literature when I read Hazlitt's *Dramatic Literature of the Age of Elizabeth* at the age of fifteen. Other people speak of Shakespeare but I had fenced since I was eight and the Bellario who drew her sword and fought was a part of my youth. She was neither afraid of death nor of fighting and she was loyal. I much preferred her to Viola and Rosalind who were scared of their weapons.

"What is this?" I asked when Kenneth Maggs returned.

"Oh, that's a nice copy of the first quarto."

I gazed at it in awe, feeling that I ought not to have touched it and out of curiosity asked the price. I supposed such books to be worth hundreds of pounds and their destiny a museum. It was true that a friend of my father had once shown me an Elizabethan grammar with little sketches of boys in ruffs and trunk hose in the margin but that had been many years previously, its owner was a scholar, and it had been a school book, not a play.

"Fifteen guineas," he said cheerfully and then added, noticing my surprise, "Beaumont and Fletcher are not collected much nowadays."

"And is it really *Philaster*?"

"Yes, it's even got the title page; sometimes they've been taken out."

I ventured to pat the book delicately.

"Look at it if you want to," he said and I turned the pages to speeches that when I was fifteen I had learned by heart.

"Would you hold it for me while I go to the bank and get the money? We never keep much in the house with all these raids."

"Is it a London bank?"

"Yes." I told him the name.

"Then I'll take a check. It will save both of us time."

I had difficulty in writing it out, I was so afraid. You can't go into a bookshop, I thought, and walk away with an Elizabethan play. I had assumed, because I venerated my Elizabethans and could never understand why my appreciation of them was so little shared, that if copies of the first editions existed, they were locked up in libraries and available only to scholars.

Possession brought responsibility. I thought of raids and arranged for the book to be stored in the country "for the duration." I got a few other less fashionable Elizabethan books during the subsequent years but after the war passed them on to scholars who could make good use of them. I have no objection to collecting but you cannot have both an Elizabethan library and adventure, and I knew which I preferred. Besides, I had no technical qualifications although both Kenneth Maggs and Gerald Henderson tried to teach me to read Elizabethan script. "A little practice and it's easy," Mr. Maggs said, "it's different with inks. They took me four months." Being of Quaker stock, he approved my decision to send the volumes where they were valuable for research. To cheer the dark wartime days he provided me instead with a series of travel diaries at little cost that had been written by intrepid Victorian ladies who had traveled across India or Darkest Africa in rows of petticoats, quelling mutinies with their umbrellas.

Still, merely having touched my Elizabethans sent me back to that age and to the research that resulted finally in writing *The Player's Boy*.

The England for which we fought was killed by bureaucracy, not war.

The book of the moment was unquestionably *The Red Tapeworm* by Compton Mackenzie. It was a perfect expression of the frustration that we all felt. We wanted to do useful work but all that happened was incompetence, delay and the apparently deliberate placing of square pegs in round holes.

The bombs came down at night and we fought the petty and meaningless restrictions imposed on us with Blitz-ruffled nerves during the day. Then, with superb timing, *The Red Tapeworm* spread from one end of London to another. We quoted it to each other standing in the queues and sometimes during questioning by some particularly obtuse official.

I think Hilda wrote to Compton Mackenzie first but afterwards I was able to send him the latest news about our mutual friend, Norman Douglas, and he and his wife, Faith, asked us up to their house on Barra. Hilda could not leave London but I accepted the invitation and it was then that my own "Red Tapeworm" saga began.

Barra was in a restricted area for which permits were essential but it was evidently part of the security arrangements that nobody could tell me where such a document could be obtained. Finally I went on June 9th to Euston Station because most of the trains for Scotland left from there and they advised me at the ticket office to make an application in writing to their Passenger Agent.

On June 11th, I received a letter saying that my application had been forwarded to the Passport Office.

On June 14th, two forms and a leaflet of instructions arrived by the morning post. The leaflet stated that the forms must be filled up and sent with an official document of identity to one of three officers whose addresses were listed.

I went the same day to have a passport photograph taken and the forms verified by an official who knew me personally. What happened to the wretched individuals who might have been drafted to work in London, had relatives in the Hebrides, and did not know any officials, was not noted. I had some difficulty in filling up the papers because when asked to state the object of my visit, I felt it might be unwise to put "to discuss the inefficiency of the present rationing system with an expert," so for once I was cautious. I entered my name, address, date and place of birth, employment and the day I wished to leave (how could I know this till I got the permit?) and then sat on hard benches in dreary waiting rooms for more hours than I could count. (It was, however, a superb training for writing *Visa to Avalon*.) On June 18th, my green identity card with attached photograph arrived, and—following the directive—I took it with my two forms to the Passport Office. I was receiving constant letters from Compton Mackenzie who was expecting other visitors and naturally wanted to know the date of my arrival. I explained the situation and asked if it was possible to expedite the issue of the permit. They replied I should have sent in the forms at once and brought in the identity card afterwards although there was a notice in the leaflet expressly forbidding this action. Finally an official asked me so many absurd questions that had nothing to do with Barra that I told him, I hope gently, exactly what I thought about Civil Service organization. "Perhaps you would like to put that down in writing?" he inquired icily, expecting me to be frightened. "Oh, yes, do let's waste another sheet of paper" was my delighted reply. After crossing France with the threat of being sent to a camp for enemy aliens hanging over my head, Tapeworms held no terrors for me. I was about to begin a dissertation upon the to-be-hoped-for reform of his office when he snorted, "Your request will have to pass through the usual channels and you will be informed later if it is granted."

I sighed and asked the officer whether if there were an invasion, the Germans would announce the event in triplicate upon the appropriate forms?

He shrugged his shoulders and indicated the door.

On the 4th of July, I hope in tribute to Independence Day in America, my permit arrived.

By that time there was a chance to take Hilda briefly to Cornwall and so it was only in September, nearly a year to the day since I had arrived from Switzerland, that I started for Scotland.

There was an air-raid warning when I got to the station but the "all clear" sounded just as the train left. The journey as far as the border passed without incident but I had to change at a junction the next morning, I do not know which it was because all the names of the stations were removed in wartime and the conductor startled me by saying, "We're running half an hour late, madam,

you may just make the train but are you sure it is running? It's Sunday."

I had forgotten that the Sabbath was so rigidly enforced in Scotland but I had had full instructions from
the Mackenzies and they had suggested weekend travel.
The steamer to Barra only went twice a week and I spent
the next hour looking gloomily at my watch. I was already inside a restricted area where I should not be permitted to remain and it would be so ignominious to be
sent back to London. Besides, what was I going to do if
there were no trains? Fortunately the one to Oban had
waited for our arrival at the junction, it was running although it was a Sunday, and once I knew I was bound for
the right port, I settled down to enjoy the landscape of
green, low hills.

I hardly knew Scotland at all. I had spent three weeks
at Edinburgh with my parents as a child and it had
rained every day but one during our stay. My only other
visit was marine and vivid. We had made a summer trip
by steamer from Dunkirk to Glasgow. I remembered
Dunkirk as a sleepy French port full of gardens belong-
ing to sea captains and little bridges from which we
looked down at the reflections of the trees in slowly moving water. It seemed a place that had exhausted itself
during the great voyages of the eighteenth century and
had since sunk into a dream. It was different when we
steamed north through the wild beauty of the Pentland
Firth and then, rocking enough to make me fear the unut-
terable disgrace of being seasick, we had continued
slowly down the West Coast. The voyage had taken three

days. One night, after we were in calmer water, the son of a passenger had sprung up after dinner and recited *The Wreck of the Hesperus* to us with great emotion. Instead of appreciating the chance to share an antique piece of Victoriana, I was both embarrassed and shocked! Later to my family's disbelief and my own annoyance I had slept calmly through the noise of a foghorn sounding right above my bunk as we had crept through the inevitable fog into the harbor.

We reached Oban eventually and I boarded the steamer that evening. My bunk was in a stateroom occupied by several other women, it was cold so we got into dressing gowns but did not otherwise undress. Being a trained traveler I was already asleep when the security officer began his rounds. He flashed a powerful torch at our faces and identity cards; permits and tickets were then carefully checked. No sooner had we gone to sleep than the process was repeated. Two of us happened to have the same surname beginning with Mac, not an unlikely occurrence in Scotland but this awakened the officer's direst suspicions and he came back with his superior a third time. "Why do you want to go to Barra?" he asked. "To see friends," I pushed my formal invitation from the Mackenzies into his hand. He stared at it so hard that I wondered if after crossing Europe safely I was going to be arrested at home? He looked at my identity card again, handed me back my papers and went on to the next bunk. It was occupied by a native islander and she shouted at him. Finally, a row of yellow faces and crumpled gray dressing gowns, we were left in peace. It seemed an appropriate introduction to the "Tapeworm's" creator.

I had sat for hours on the sands in Cornwall but I had not actually been at sea for a couple of years so I went on deck directly after breakfast in the morning. The Sound was full of small, black trawlers tossing on very blue waves. I found a sheltered seat but a woman who could only be described as "bustling" immediately sat down beside me and introduced herself as a clergyman's wife. I was glad it was a Monday. Where was I going? What did I do? I replied that I was visiting some friends and she said in return that she was going to her relatives in, I think it was, Tiree. "I hope we shall not be more than two hours late," she continued cheerfully, "it's tiresome for them having to wait on the pier."

"Late!" I snatched my letter out of my bag. "According to my instructions, I am due at Barra at four."

"Four! You can't go by any old timetable. We stop a dozen times to unload passengers and stores. You'll be lucky if you get to Castle Bay by midnight."

Why had I been foolish enough to come north at all? It is simply "not done" to dump one's self on complete strangers, however welcoming their letters, in the middle of the night.

I was distracted from these apprehensions by an airplane flying rather low above our heads and with the instinctive reaction of all Londoners, I glanced up to see what it was. "It's British," a passenger said reassuringly as he walked past.

"Do you pray for the Germans during the raids?" the

clergyman's wife asked me to my extreme astonishment. "I do," she said, "I pray for those poor German boys. We are all sinners." Perhaps we were, but having seen both tortured refugees and bombed-out friends, I could only answer angrily, "Do you *know* what they did to their own people?"

"Oh, the reports were exaggerated, you know; you mustn't believe all you read in the newspapers."

"But the truth, the truth as I saw it, was never even reported. I worked with the refugees for seven years."

"Unfortunate mistakes can happen but then we must redouble our prayers. I assure you, if the Germans landed I should make no effort to resist them."

Such attitudes are typical of people who are able to control their own aggression only by repressing it and they amount to a rejection of humanity in all the meanings of the word. To be able to shock others with their unpopular views gives them an unacknowledged feeling of power. They conceal a driving sense of domination under an apparent humility but they are incapable of sympathy or love. Unfortunately so many of them gain a position where they have children under their control and thus leave behind them a trail of wrecked lives. Silence is always better at such moments so I did not reply but after a few moments got up and walked away to another seat.

It was a day, they usually mark the end of summer, when the waves were crisp with sparks of light rather than spray. I wished, as we do so often when it is too late, that I had gone to sea more frequently during the Peace.

At least it gave one an illusion of freedom. Every two hours or so we stopped at some port to land boxes, barrels and finally, to everyone's delight, the clergyman's wife. Perhaps it was imagination but I did not feel that the group that came towards her was noisy with enthusiasm. "Don't worry," a fellow passenger said, whenever he saw me looking at my watch, "your friends at Barra will expect you to be late."

In spite of the security precautions the voyage was the nearest approach to peace that I had known for two years. I stayed on deck until the cold and the darkness drove me finally into the lounge. At intervals we were fed. I was sleepy by the time that we got to Castle Bay at ten o'clock that night but a man came up at once and asked me if I were the visitor for the Mackenzies? It was easy for him to recognize me, all the other passengers were natives of the island. I apologized for the delay, he reassured me by saying that in wartime this was anticipated; then he led me to a car and disappeared. I wondered again as I sat there in totally unfamiliar surroundings precisely why I had come? Suddenly the driver returned, he pressed a packet of cigarettes into my hand, and remarked that I must need one after the journey. Actually I seldom smoked, but they were extremely scarce at the time and I shall always remember his gesture of Highland kindness. He had never seen me before, he was waiting for his call-up papers and I never found out his name. But I was a stranger and I knew he wanted to welcome me to his island.

And so I came to Suidheachen. Nobody who saw the

house could ever forget it. It was on one floor, modern in design, and the two long wings seemed to rise directly from the fine white sand. Faith met me at the door, I was briefly introduced to Monty who was in bed with an attack of his recurring sciatica and then left to sleep off the effects of a rather peculiar journey in a room that to my delight reminded me of a cabin.

Some gladiator with net and trident seemed always at hand to loop me back to a not-so-distant past. The following morning I was left in Monty's library and immediately discovered a row of books on early Scottish history. By chance I opened a volume on trade during the early Middle Ages and discovered that ten thousand Scottish traders at that time traveled regularly in Poland or along the Baltic Coast. Naturally the Street of the Merchants at Riga flashed immediately across my mind. What had happened to the people I had seen on a journey through Latvia, Estonia and Finland in 1939? My own friends had managed to get to America on the last steamer to leave before the war but what about the others I had met for an hour or so and who had been so kind to me? I seemed to smell a mingled scent of pines and sand on the "amber beaches" that I had never smelt anywhere else, until Faith arrived to show me the rest of the house.

Looking back today, I wonder what Faith can have made of me on that first visit? All we had in common was our friendship with Norman Douglas and somehow that led our conversation immediately to Capri. It helped her that I had visited the island several times because it was the core of her life. If only she could have stayed there. There are people it is wise never to transplant. She loved Monty but he was a born wanderer, a conqueror of islands rather than a settler. She had just been in time to see the final years of that famous English colony that had all but ruled the place and was at its most masterful about 1905. What a strange world it must have been with its mixture of license and Victorian propriety. It was extraordinary to look at some old photographs and realize that the women in them with their long skirts and enormous hats had already stamped their names upon the art of their time. Yet, unlike the transients of today, those residents were firmly rooted in the island's soil. It amused me to remember that I had visited that Capri myself, if only for a day, when I was eight, and how often in later years I had looked down from the rocks at that same blue sea that can have changed so little since the lava covered Pompeii. Later Norman Douglas had even taken me to see John Ellingham Brooks who had given me his translations of French poetry to read and I had known Romaine Brooks, his wife, the artist, and Natalie Barney in France. I had had some contact therefore, with Faith's world (her *Afternoon Memories* is one of the few true records of it) but now with so many friends vanished we did not know where, all seemed lost.

How hard it is to make absent friends live again. Memory is not merely a matter of words. It is sights, sounds, impressions, distinct but not continuous, an isolated word with a blank on either side of it. Ours is an archaeologist's duty to decipher a few letters here or a whole word there from a text that has worn away. Faith was older than I was and we came from dissimilar generations. She was late Victorian by inclination whereas I belonged to the Twenties, to a tougher world where the first lesson was never to express an unnecessary emotion. I wished immediately that she could have met my mother. What friends they might have become! They had so much in common.

I rarely saw Monty before evening. His attack of sciatica continued but at night he was able to read some chapters from a novel he had just finished, *The Monarch of the Glen,* and I have seldom had so hilarious an experience. He was able to give the accent, the nuance of each Highland word that a foreigner, especially if Saxon, could not know. I particularly appreciated one character, Carrie, struggling with her Gaelic because I have an awkward habit myself of carrying a phrase book of some strange language about with me, usually getting blocked at Lesson Five. We needed to laugh because the fog was getting denser over Europe and my chances of ever returning to Burier remote.

After Monty had finished reading, he talked about the war or politics until long after midnight. He had been writing on *Gallipoli* and spoke most of the evenings about his own experience there. It may be that it is the artist rather than the historian who has the vision to give certain moments of the national chronicle their full and terrible value. Certainly he was uttering a dirge of England although I could not admit it till long afterwards. "When the country regiments were sent in to what we knew was a useless slaughter, England, as we had known it, was totally destroyed." Monty was not speaking then in a narrow political sense, and some of the words he used have different meanings today. In each age a majority conforms to a certain tradition yet often makes use of what were to a previous generation revolutionary terms. The outcry about pollution of the earth today is not unlike what was meant by patriotism in 1910. When the blacksmith's boy and the squire's son died together at Gallipoli, they both shared a belief in certain values that are incomprehensible to the present generation because the meaning of the words has changed. The great difficulty for historians is to find out what a certain sentence really meant in a particular year. Nothing is as unstable as speech; misunderstanding of what an earlier generation really meant is so easy as to be almost inevitable.

I have known many islands but I have seldom been on one as wild as Barra. As I watched the waves hurling themselves against the rocks or spreading across the white shore that was so different from my Scillonian gold, I felt I was stealing some days back from winter. One day Faith came out to call me. "Listen," she said, "this does not happen very often. An islander went to work at a factory in Glasgow and died there. His body has been brought back for burial to his native place." We could hear the pipers as the coffin was carried across the sands. I have no feeling for music but I would go anywhere to hear the pipes; they must awake some race memory in the blood because they give me a feeling of eternity that I have never heard in any other sound.

The week for which I had been invited passed all too quickly, yet lovely as Barra was, nobody could have failed to notice a tension in the house. I do not know if it is an advantage or not to see both sides of a situation (it is always uncomfortable), but I know from personal experience that it is rare for intense love to last an equal length of time between two people. We think it must endure for eternity; it is as ephemeral as a butterfly. Once it cools it may pass into deep affection but the original glory is lost and whatever love is, it is not reason. Such a moment had come between Monty and Faith. They said little but I could feel it without being told. It was agreed that Faith should return with me to London. Barra was too wild and alien a place for her and she had gone there only for Monty's sake. Her roots, if not in Capri were at least in the English South where she had been born.

Our trip was easier because she knew the tricks of the journey and she stayed with us for a short time at Lowndes until she could move into a little house she owned at Hampstead where she remained for much of the war.

1942

1942 was what I called my Friendship and Persian year.

The war was having a bad effect upon my morale and the petty restrictions increased. Each day represented an epoch of the Glacial Age and I am never at my best when I am cold. We had snow, some bad raids and I described what I felt in a letter to a friend in America, dated February 8th. It was usual to keep carbons of our letters if we wrote overseas because so much of the mail was lost.

"I proceeded this morning with the utmost caution over ice to get our food for the day. 'Oh, madam, is it thawing?' a cleaning woman inquired to whom I could only reply, 'No, it's the worst day I remember.' I walked on into Sloane Street and inquired sympathetically after the feet of the fire watcher and contributed a small donaion towards a pair of rubbers.

"Naturally we do not dress for dinner but we are firm. We do not wear our hot-water bottles to table. The worst of it is, I am afraid to sit on mine as they cannot be replaced. However, *Hansard* arrived with a glorious report of a Government debate as to the virility of *Vogue*."

Osbert had suggested that I subscribe to *Hansard* and it was excellent advice. It was the only publication to contain some genuine news and it also offered some of the few hilarious moments of the war. There appeared to be a serious account of some proposal to train sea lions to spot mines. I could not continue my subscription to it after I returned home in 1946 because there is no time to peruse it during ordinary life.

I had also reason to be very grateful to him with regard to another matter. My legal situation was extremely complicated because I had been domiciled in Switzerland since 1923 and had to sign every document "temporarily by Act of God in England." My father's lawyer whom I had always consulted was elderly and now retired. I asked Osbert for advice and he introduced me to his advisor, Philip Frere. Mr. Frere immediately joined our Lowndes Group, gave me invaluable advice and it was due to his efforts that I was among the first of the exiles to be able to return home in 1946. It was not

merely legal counsel but he was gay and witty throughout the blackest moments of the final raids and like
myself saw no reason to placate the bureaucrats and their
regulations because of a war that we had foreseen must
happen but that they had ignored until it was almost too
late.

I began to be worried about my morale. I patted it, I
fed it the nicest morsels I could find, for who would collect the rations if I cracked? To restore myself, I wondered what was the most *useless* thing I could do? I decided to learn Persian.

Why Persian? Because, my masters, at such a time of
utter despair we fall back on childhood and that to me
meant galloping in complete freedom across the desert.
Those days had been dreaming come alive and I have
read since in many biographies that children who had
had similar experiences to my own were marked by them
for life. We all looked at events afterwards from a
slightly different angle to our western fellows. At ten I
had absorbed the atmosphere in a manner impossible to
the adult, reflective mind. I had returned to the Orient
when I was thirty but by then I was conscious only of the
virtual slavery inflicted on its women and had no wish to
remain. A child is unconscious of such problems.

I also discovered E. G. Browne's magnificent *Literary
History of Persia*. It became my constant companion
during the war because it was less the literature that interested me than the repetition of a story. A civilization
rose. It would not listen to the wise, it neglected its own
protection and was overrun and destroyed by the barbar-

ians. The circumstances were repeated several times and was it not just what had happened to us in 1940? It was far more helpful to face this when the mind needed solace (will the war never end?) than to murmur the official exhortation, "Britain can take it." I had always wanted to apply a knowledge of the past to a vision of the future and I owe to E. G. Browne a fear of China that I have felt with growing intensity since 1942.

Persian, therefore, became my wartime talisman and I bought some Linguaphone records cheaply because nobody wanted them. Progress was slow, however, so I decided to find a teacher.

The School of Oriental Languages had been taken over "for the duration" and was extremely suspicious about my inquiry. Was my interest in Persian really necessary? After some prodding, they eventually produced an address and thus I became Mrs. Waite's last pupil. She must have been almost eighty, thin, rather tall and the daughter of English missionaries who had settled in a Persian village when she was a baby, owning a Bible but hardly any funds. I could never discover the precise Protestant sect to which the family had belonged. It cannot have been an easy life for a child, "It was the dogs, dear, they were so savage that I was never allowed to play outside alone," but week by week throughout the year a small coin was set aside so that they could have the traditional plum pudding at Christmas. The summers had been dry and they had not always had enough water, the winters bitterly cold. Oh, why must people think of

flags and parades when they speak of the empire? It is
not the truth at all. We shall be remembered in the East
because of the English from tenements and small provin-
cial towns who crossed the Indian Ocean to work in
stores, on railways, on leaky coastal steamers or as missionaries and teachers. Their incomes were low, there
was no great gap between them and the people they were
serving and most of them never lived to go home. They
managed letters but were seldom literate enough to pro-
duce a book yet through them something of the East got
into the English soul and it is a matter of profound regret
to the historian that the material necessary to write their
story has now been irretrievably destroyed.

If a verb got too tricky, I turned Mrs. Waite's attention
to her girlhood but I learned to repeat that a house had a
garden and a door, to count up to ten and to try unsuc-
cessfully to pronounce the letter *qaf*. "It does help, naturally, if you are used to camels but try the sound again.
Cough, dear, cough." She worried about the state of my
soul and why I should want to learn the language? I had
to hint (it had once been suggested to me) that I might be
offered a post there to help in the Polish refugee camps.
She could accept such a possibility but not that learning
Persian in wartime might be only for fun. Her parents
had frightened her so thoroughly about the sinfulness of
lying that if she thought she had erred in explaining a
grammatical rule, she apologized for ten minutes. She
had also become a Christian Scientist and that was less
than helpful when she arrived with a cold that she passed

on to me and I, in turn, to Hilda. "Oh, Bryher," Hilda grumbled from behind a handkerchief, "must you always have more enthusiasm than sense?"

My own opinion was that Persian was a proper employment for my brief spare time. The important thing was less that I never acquired a proper guttural growl than that my lessons impelled me to read book after book about the history of the Near East. Nobody wanted them in 1942 so I picked up volumes like Gibbs' *History of Ottoman Poetry* and Browne's marvelous *A Year in Persia* for a few shillings instead of pounds. I saw our world through the barbarian invasions of the past and I studied these volumes not to escape but to understand our extremely difficult present of gunfire and crashes.

I felt no particular alarm during the early raids. Why should I? I had been inoculated against fear during my work with the refugees. I have never been able to make people understand that I had earlier suffered such paralyzing terror that bombs seemed simple in comparison. How much danger I was in during the prewar years I do not know but my only protection had been a bit of blue cardboard, my English passport. My friends had risked torture, it might have been extended to myself and I had doubted if I could hold out under it; some had been beaten and all had had to leave homes, libraries, the environment that had grown round them since childhood for an unknown and uncertain future. Now if an alert went, I was for the moment a Londoner and "London could take it."

So we had our moment, the Persian language and myself. A warning sounded but I was close to the *Life and Letters* office and saw no reason to take shelter. Something seemed to explode above my head (it was probably miles away) and I lost my temper, as much with the Appeasers as the enemy. How dared they drive me out of my home through their stupidity and fanaticism and subject me to the thousand anxieties and discomforts of a second war? *"Qaf,"* I yelled in my most guttural voice, *"qaf,"* and I followed this with four lines of an old Persian poem that I had learned with great toil. Nobody among the passers-by seemed to find my behavior strange. At least, I felt, I had shown "them all" that to know was more important than to threaten. "One of these days you will get arrested," was a friend's unfeeling comment when I got to the office. "Nobody will know that you are trying to talk Persian. They will think you are signaling to the enemy."

Now, alas, after all my struggles with the language I cannot remember a word of it and I have refused two invitations to visit Teheran during the last ten years. It was purely an antidote but an antidote that got me through some very difficult years and I obtained, at least, a knowledge of the history of the Near East that I might never have had otherwise. It is something that I can never rub out because it goes back to a fulfillment of all a child's desires. After the war, when I went briefly to Pakistan, I was still torn between some inward recognition and a surface strangeness but by then I knew that I was rooted firmly in the West.

Mrs. Waite eventually moved away from London so

my lessons came to an end but we corresponded regularly with each other until she died shortly after the war.

Camels, however, seemed to haunt me. I opened the newspaper one April morning to find that the Zoo was offering to sell clippings from their coats without coupons. Our clothes by now were wearing out but even Robert was uninterested although he was temporarily in London getting his bomb-damaged house repaired, so I dashed off alone at lunch hour. The Gardens were forlorn and the doorkeeper looked at me suspiciously when I asked him for a ticket. Fortunately I had cut the announcement carefully out of the paper and I showed it to him. "Oh, papers, you know . . . ," he shrugged his shoulders with the innate distrust of most English for the printed word but he indicated the direction of the Camel House before resuming his study of the empty, outer road.

I was obviously the only visitor and it was a little lonely walking along the formerly crowded paths in front of two zebras, a demonstration enclosure full of pigs and a couple of chattering monkeys. Once I had ridden on a real camel across hot sand. Once one had tried to bite me. People prized their camel-hair coats. If the war went on my enterprise in following up the information might win me a fortune. Be bold, I thought, don't let the Establishment get you down, try anything once. I should have remembered a dozen other slogans but by then I had reached my destination. The Head Keeper was

out but they would fetch, they promised me, Assistant
Camels.

I waited a very long time but eventually a man arrived, looking puzzled but otherwise affable. Yes, he assured me, they combed the beasts regularly to keep their
coats from becoming matted and a firm had previously
collected these combings, he did not know for what purpose, could it have been for brushes? "I've got two sacks
of Droms and five of Bacs." He meant, I presumed,
Dromedaries and Bactrians but how impolite, even in
wartime, not to refer to his charges by their full names.
No, the animals had not minded the raids but oh, how
they hated storms! "Naturally," I replied, remembering
my camel-minded childhood, "a wind in the Sahara fills
their coats full of dust."

"Had I a bag?"

In my enthusiasm I had forgotten this precaution.

Well, he would see what he could do. He hailed a
friend and left me alone with the animals. They ignored
me. It seemed ages before he returned with a sack full of
combings and then he actually helped me to find a taxi at
the gate.

"Stinks, it does!" The driver slammed a window shut
and we charged rather than proceeded decorously
through the empty streets to Lowndes Square.

"You can't keep that stuff here," was Hilda's unenthu-
siastic reception, "see if they will let you store it in the
basement."

"But it's camel and off coupons."

Hilda slammed the door and it was only after much discussion that I was able to find a corner for my sack at the side of the baggage room. People would not realize that if conditions got worse I was a public benefactor. Finally I rang up Cole, who greeted me with inordinate and I felt misplaced laughter. "But wool like that is too harsh, it will have to be carded and washed and you can't do that yourself in London but I'll give you the address of a friend. She weaves cloth and I think she collects sheep clippings sometimes from the hedges."

In due course a letter came from Cole but whenever I was free her friend was at work so that it was almost a week before I obtained the address of a firm in the Hebrides and longer still until they agreed to accept the combings. Meantime I heard a resident at Lowndes complaining about a curious smell in the basement, could it be the new gas? I got Mrs. Ash to help me pack the clippings inside paper that we had drenched with disinfectant and posted them to Scotland. I heard no more for six months. Then without warning six skeins of rough and prickly wool, together with a startlingly small bill arrived with the morning post.

Our winter clothes were already thin with wear but I cannot pretend that the wool was a success. I shared it eventually with Osbert. He had a coat made that he gave later to a gamekeeper, then doing night watches. I have always felt the cold terribly but my jacket was too hot even for me and I passed it on to a farming friend to wear during the lambing season.

Still I do not regret the expedition. What is man if he

does not take chances? Besides, it is not everyone who can boast of carrying camel clippings to a London home. It is only sad to reflect that good intentions so frequently lead to negative results.

I still wonder if the Renishaw I knew during the war ever existed? Or was it another of the strange islands found by the early voyagers, never seen again after they left, existing only in their songs? In retrospect, the light was always gold, the words an oracle, with Osbert the sage and Edith the skald. I believed that the patches of wild pansies and the milkworts were an enamel set in the grass and that I should never find afterwards our favorite meadow near a stream and below a little wood.

I loved my visits because in London I was up against a curious taboo. Only Osbert allowed me to speak about Burier although it had been my home for many years and my books, my dogs, Elsie and many friends I valued were still there and I heard from them if I were lucky, perhaps once in a year. I did not want to grumble, I only wanted to talk about it occasionally without coming up against a glacial silence. I felt my friends should realize that I had returned to stand beside them in the "shield wall" rather than from feeling a need otherwise to come back to England. Osbert had Montegufoni, I had Burier, and it helped us both, I think, to remember a lost paradise. There was no false hopefulness in our talk. Whatever Osbert may have written about it, his Guard's training had not been in vain. He looked at the situation in Europe as if he were standing himself inside the plan-ning room for a campaign. Nor did he ever suggest that there could be a quick or easy ending much as I longed for comfort. "It will be seven years or longer, but we have our duty, to preserve what we can of art." I hoped he was wrong but dismally in my heart I knew that he was right. (It was actually six years and a half.) Of all the people I met, he and he alone, saw the struggle in perspective and understood what might happen when peace came. England would change, some art would survive, but when it would be possible to write freely again, he did not know. Then calmly as to voice but with a veiled despair he would ask, "Do you think, Bryher, I am right?" All I could do was to say "Yes" while I was praying for him to give me some hope that the end of the war was near even if it were only an illusion. Only that would have been the unpardonable sin, not to have seen clearly or perceive ahead what was likely to happen in a postwar world.

Whenever I think of Edith, it is summer at Renishaw. We seldom obeyed Osbert's instructions to sit out of doors but stayed instead, just inside the doorway that led to the terrace above the formal beds that I had once seen bright with flowers but now were full of vegetables. There Edith used to read to me Shakespeare, the old ballads and if I pleaded very hard, her own poems. Her voice, the air, an ornament on her dress, all seemed golden while the landscape beyond us hovered in the cool Derbyshire sunshine as if a giant butterfly were protecting the grass with its coral and amber wings.

Edith had less hope than Osbert about the future but it

made her the more determined to create what we had lost, an Elizabethan sense of courage and beauty. Poetry to her was as the nun's dedication in the Middle Ages and she tolerated no pretense. Perhaps this was the reason that she had so many enemies. Only the few who have reached a certain stage of development can understand so pure a devotion. It was also a jealous feeling of guardianship. H.D. had it as well but Hilda was more philosophical. She knew that the Golden Age would never recur but that memories might come back from it. Something of it had also enabled me to break away from tradition and home and saved me, oddly enough, from a few of the real dangers of the Paris Twenties. Yet I never understood why Edith admitted me into the inner circle of her friendship except that she knew I was conscious of what she was trying to do. Others to whom she read her poems were able to find the right words to demonstrate their gratitude. I had been trained to silence and could only feel. Perhaps Edith knew instinctively that I understood her even if I were powerless to thank her in words.

All of us have our assigned tasks and mine was to be a messenger. Only there are lines today that I can never read again because both Edith's and Hilda's voices are now lost to me.

There were other aspects of Renishaw. Everything was done even in wartime to make a visitor comfortable but it had been built for a giant race. It would have been taken over "for the duration" by the Government but there was no electricity and it could not be installed without almost rebuilding the house. The rooms were lit either by candles or lamps. It was not a place to go down to dinner with one's hair standing on end but I am very short whereas all the Sitwells were tall. Even if I dared risk standing on an antique and valuable stool, the mirror was one side of the room and the lamp on the other. I used to go downstairs feeling that I was about to attend one of the alarming evenings at school when we were inspected as we entered the drawing room. "Whatever interests you in that picture?" Edith would ask. "It's not one of our better ones." It reflected a light however and I would try frantically to think of some artistic explanation while straightening my collar and smoothing down a stray hair. How often problems of life hinge upon such apparently unimportant details.

I did not always stay at Renishaw when I went to Derbyshire. Robert Herring had rented a house at Eckington, the next village, until his house in Chelsea that had been badly damaged by a bomb could be repaired. He had moved the files and much of the material for *Life and Letters* there for safety. He was most generous about inviting friends for a weekend away from the grime of London and I went down about twice a year to discuss plans and take manuscripts back from there to the office. To repeat, we sold every copy we had enough paper to print and we were even making a profit. I fear this was due to two reasons: soldiers in the training camps snatched at any magazine they could find and as advertising was so restricted in the Press in general, we were offered more than we could accept. It was a lesson that "little magazines" seem needed only at a time of national catastrophe. We also suffered from an irritating experience. Both Herring and I had known that the war was coming and we had bought a large stock of paper in 1938. This was prescience and wisdom. It was now suggested that we were hoarding and part of our store, acquired long before the outbreak of war, was deflected towards our rivals. It was one more example of the muddle and ineptitude of the official departments. Foresight was penalized and the ostrich rewarded.

We used to take long walks through the forest to calm our anger. It was a different period and landscape from my so-loved Cornwall, more medieval in atmosphere; Herring and I often felt that if we had seen the leather sleeve of an archer disappearing past a tree trunk we should not have been surprised. The paths were thick with fallen leaves even in summer and once we came out on an open field that was so thick with miniature pansies that it really resembled a Persian carpet. Yet lovely and exciting as it was, I felt an obscure uneasiness, it was almost shame, that I was not in London. However legitimate our absence might be, we all felt it when we were away from our city.

The hero of my childhood was Sir Richard Burton. It was inevitable that, in the modern phrase, I should identify myself with him. He had had a supremely happy childhood wandering about Europe; so had I. He had been a swordsman and I had never been happier than when I had a foil in my hand; he had been snatched from

his travels and flung into a hated English school as I had
been sent to Queenwood, then he had roamed the world,
speaking a score of languages as if he had been a native
of each country, and had written many books. Burton
had not imagined his adventures, he had experienced
them. It was true that except for *Al-Medinah and Mec-
cah,* the few other books by him that, aged ten, I had discovered in my uncle's library, proved extremely dull but
then, writing about an exploit is not the same as living it
and I could think of few people I more admired. To be
free to wander in a foreign land when young is one of the
greatest gifts life can offer and it always has an effect
upon later development. I recognized the truth of this
again when I read Eric Shipton's wonderful autobiography, *That Untravelled World.* The basic elements are, I
believe, the color, the strangeness and the sense of being
completely on one's own.

My Persian lessons awakened my own memories of the
East and when a new life of his wife, Isabel, by Jean
Burton came into the *Life and Letters* office, I asked to be
allowed to review it. It reopened the question of Damascus. Was it the simple matter of Hero against Establishment or was there a darker or more puzzling side to the
story than had ever been disclosed?

Burton was disliked by many people in official positions because of his unorthodox opinions. He was given
posts in two unhealthy places, one in West Africa and the
other in Brazil before he was finally appointed consul at
Damascus where his wide knowledge of Oriental languages and customs should have been of great value. Two

years later he was abruptly dismissed. The real reasons for this action have never been fully explained. Burton was hated by the Turkish Wali then in charge who was himself recalled to Constantinople a short time afterwards on account of his intrigues; the British Ambassador at Constantinople disliked him, there were several curious incidents when he and his wife were attacked whilst making journeys and compelled to beat off their assailants by force. Probably the major cause was the attempt by Isabel Burton to protect the Druses and convert some tribesmen to Christianity. It was some time after his recall before Burton was appointed to a minor post as consul at Trieste. He had leisure there to finish his work on the translation of *The Thousand Nights and a Night* and some other classics but his career in the East was over.

Yet what had really happened? There were hints but no facts. A Blue Book was said to exist on the subject but I combed the shelves of the London Library in vain. Eventually Robert suggested writing to Sir Stephen Gaselee at the Foreign Office to find out where it could be obtained?

Sir Stephen replied a few days later. If we had a real reason for wishing to see the document in question, we could call on him at the Foreign Office at a certain date and time and read it at his office.

I think I have seldom been more alarmed. A policeman, treating Robert and myself as if we were two lost children at the Zoo, led us along one corridor after another, all stacked with the inevitable sandbags, until we reached Sir Stephen's room. He did not put us at our ease, he looked us up and down, it was plain that he considered us intruders as indeed we were, then he growled (but is growl the right word for that ominously glacial sound that seems to erupt naturally from the throats of highly placed officials), "Why, precisely, do you wish to consult this document?"

Normally I should have answered boldly, "Because Burton was a rebel and the best swordsman of his age" but I realized that silence was golden, as they used to say to me in the nursery, and Robert hastily explained his Cambridge credentials and added that as a new biography was about to be reviewed in *Life and Letters,* we would like to check some facts.

Sir Stephen grunted again and sent for the document. While we waited he conversed with Robert about the weather, always the light matter of an English conversation. I was beginning to wonder if he suspected us of using Burton's name to penetrate the Foreign Office and blow it up when a messenger brought in a booklet so promptly that I imagine that it had already been extracted from the files. It was bound in the correct style and color of a Blue Book but Sir Stephen picked it up triumphantly, "You will note that it is *not* a Government Publication although it has been got up to look like one; it is, if this is what you wish to check, a fake."

It was, but it was a discovery that no other student of Burton appeared to have made. Alas, with Sir Stephen watching us, we had neither time to read the document slowly nor to make notes. It is still unknown to most scholars. Even Fawn Brodie who wrote a well-documented life of Burton, *The Devil Drives*, published in 1967, said she had never heard of it until I wrote her about our investigation.

It appeared to be a justification by Isabel of her share in the affair. The puzzling thing to emerge was Burton's own attitude. Had he been ignorant of what his wife was doing or had he lost himself in so many disguises that the events had seemed unimportant until it was too late? It is a question that needs to be studied by an expert on the history of the Near East during the time that the Burtons were in Damascus. All we can claim is that we actually read the pamphlet.

"Odd fellow," Sir Stephen remarked when we had finished. It was evident that he had no admiration for Burton.

"But so interesting."

He did not reply. It was obvious that there was no room inside his office for intruders. I fear we did no work that morning when we got back to our own sanctuary except to agree that the mystery was still unsolved. We had proved the document existed but what did it mean? Perhaps the secret is a simple one. Explorers and the Establishment do not mix.

The months passed but one Sunday morning in November I was glancing at the newspaper when I happened to find a notice asking for "volunteer refugees" to assemble at Chelsea Town Hall. They were needed to take part in an exercise designed to test the efficiency of the Civil Defense Service in the event of an invasion. (It seemed a little late in the day!) I doubt if I should have been interested had I not caught sight of almost the last sentence. *"Please impede the police in every possible way."*

"Hilda! They want us to aggravate the police!" I dashed into our sitting room where H.D. was taking the cover off her typewriter.

"I am not going to bail you out if you do; and remember, Robert is at Eckington."

"But it's my duty as a citizen." I read the notice again and wondered what actions would be appropriate. "I think I shall go as a foreign agent."

"Go as yourself. It's more than sufficient." (Strange how little one's talents are appreciated in the home.)

"I think I ought to make a bomb."

"How!"

"Oh, I could shovel some earth into a tin, label it *Explosive*, and drop it on the step of the Town Hall."

"Leave me in peace with my work. If you are late, I shall start lunch."

I was lucky and caught a bus to Chelsea almost immediately but fretted the whole of the journey because there had been no time to work out a proper disguise. Still I had put on my by now nondescript marketing coat, a decrepit beret all but worn through at the edges and woolen gloves with holes. The Town Hall was shut but I could hear a noisy crowd moving up from the Thames. According to the newspaper, families from Kent were to cross by the Albert Bridge and Chelsea agents were to spread "alarm and despondency" by persuading them to turn back, thus jamming the approach.

To my intense delight, the populace had taken the matter seriously, they had sleeping bags strapped like rucksacks across their shoulders, a girl in a red cap was leading a big dog and a man came towards me wheeling a pram with a baby inside it and a second child sitting on the rim. Two saucepans and a pail dangled from the handle bar and his wife followed, dragging a six-year-old by the hand and looking as glum and exhausted as if she had really fled from her home. "Oh, have you heard," I tried to appear as anxious and worried as possible, "we're to go back and cross by Battersea Bridge. That's where they've opened the canteen." They stopped for a moment, looking puzzled, then a voice shouted from behind, "Don't you believe a word of it; here, Bill, here's an enemy agent."

"Your name, please."

"*An, jehaz, nan,*" I hurled the nouns from the first page of *Simple Colloquial Persian* at my questioner.

"Oh, a foreigner, interpreter, please."

A friendly-looking man in Civil Defense uniform came in and addressed me in French. My imagination decided that he was the type who would go to night classes in the language and save up for three years to take a week's holiday in Paris. I shook my head, hoping I looked sinister, and tried to register fright.

"*Sind Sie Deutsch?*"

This was not as surprising a question as it might sound because Chelsea was full of foreign refugees but I replied, a little anxiously, with the first line of a Persian poem.

The man really knew his languages. He tried me in Italian and then in what I guessed to be Czech. My answer to both was a blank stare so he ordered me firmly to stay where I was for twenty minutes. I had been captured, I was therefore out of the game and when I left I was to go straight home.

I felt he might be curious so after he departed, I scribbled "It was Persian" on a scrap of paper and left it on the table. I was still anxious to see what was happening outside so a few minutes later I slid quietly out and went round to the King's Road. The bridge part of the "Exercise" was already over and cheerful groups of volunteer refugees were gathering at street corners. It was obvious that we had all enjoyed ourselves immensely, it was the petty restrictions so often needlessly imposed that upset our morale. I looked round for a last policeman to harass but there was not even a warden in sight so I joined two elderly ladies carrying worn shopping bags at the bus stop. "Just released," I said cheerfully. One of the few pleasant things about wartime was that you could talk to anyone standing beside you in the queue.

"And what were you trying to do?"

"Disrupt the Kentish fugitives."

"Any luck?"

"No, not really. I may have turned a couple back but then a warden grabbed me so I pretended I was a foreigner."

"Well, we are really refugees. We lived in France until the war."

"Then we are compatriots. I only got here from Switzerland in 1940."

"Did you have a rough trip?"

"Not really. The journey was exciting but waiting in Lisbon was awful."

"We missed Portugal because we got here earlier, in the winter of 1939. But oh, don't you miss your house? We were wondering this morning if we should ever see our villa again."

We were not playing "fugitives" as we stood there in the middle of the scarred doors and boarded-up windows, England had ceased to be our home. I wondered if we were the beginning of a new race that was not necessarily rooted in the country of its birth? Some of us had gone abroad to get away from the memories of childhood, others, like myself, to recover them. We kept our language and some of our traditions but London would never have the easy familiarity of the regions where we had lived. "You will go back," I had to believe that I should see Burier again, "this can't go on for ever."

"But even if they let us go, where shall we find the money? Think of the repairs with the villa empty all this time!"

"You'll manage somehow. There must be a way . . ." but would there be? The flowers would have run wild or died, the trees cut down for firewood, the rooms, if only for a time, occupied by strangers. Besides, the authorities in England treated us all as if we were either criminals or spies. They were too narrow-minded or jealous to perceive that we had been scattered across Europe as deputy ambassadors, carrying ideas or even goods to people who would never come in contact with their formal, official world.

"It's the scents we miss, throwing the windows open in the early morning and knowing the seasons by the feel of the air. And some of our shrubs had taken years to grow."

"You'll have to plant others that will come up quickly. Remember, we're an enterprising race. Where else but in England should we be asked to turn out and harass the police in the middle of a war?"

"Come and have a cup of tea with us and we'll show you photographs of the villa." Tea was the one solace and it was indeed a sacrifice to offer a portion of their small ration to a stranger. I longed to accept and hear why they had gone abroad, it would be sharing the comradeship of an identical experience and I had always been fascinated by the little colonies of "England in Europe" that seemed to have existed even in Elizabethan times. I was afraid, however, that for all her scorn, Hilda might fret if I were really late.

"I wish I could but I must get back to my cousin or she may wonder if she ought to ring up the police station." My bus came along at that moment and I jumped aboard while we shouted our hopes that the war and its regulations would soon be over.

"It was glorious, Hilda, glorious," I yelled as soon as

I got through the front door, "think of it! I was even arrested."

"Naturally. How old do you think you are? Now sit down and eat your lunch. I don't want to hear a word about what happened till afterwards. I am only surprised that you came back at all."

1943

Poetry, the battle of the ration books, increasing gloom, these made up the year.

Whatever the news, the day had its welcome brightness whenever Osbert telephoned that he was in London and would I like to join him for a walk? He rang me up in February and asked me to meet him. We wandered at first across the park in such complete silence that I wondered if the war was going so badly that he dared not talk about it? Presently he stopped and looked round at the bare flower beds and wet grass. "How is Hilda?" he asked.

"Fair. She is working but things are not exactly gay, are they?"

"The time has come to do something to keep the arts alive. I have decided to organize a Poets' Reading. Do you think Hilda will help us?"

"I'm sure she will if you ask her. If I suggest it, she'll say no." (I was supposed to have too much enthusiasm and not enough perception.) "You'll have to talk to her yourself."

"I shall ask each poet to write something new for the occasion."

"Hilda has been working on something for weeks. She seldom shows me anything before it is printed." I had learned some sharp lessons about never interrupting her. "And she reads superbly."

"The Queen has consented to be Patroness."

"Oh, that will make the day for Hilda. She is always trying to balance her two nationalities." As I have written, it is foolish to belong to two countries because that always means a tug of war. Three are ideal, then one can stand aloof in what I maintain to be calmness of judgment.

"There is no need for Hilda to be nervous. Edith will read and at least a dozen others. Eliot has accepted and I've asked Masefield but with him there is a little trouble about ducks."

"Ducks, Osbert?"

"It seems they have to be fed at a certain time and he has to be there to do it. Naturally there are very few trains. Do you happen to remember if their feeding time is before or after sunset?"

All I could recall at that moment was a fragment of a nursery rhyme about their being stuffed with sage. It had greatly disturbed me as a child when we had passed some ducklings regularly on a walk. "No, but Doris has a farm. I'll write and ask her."

"Morale is low at the moment." Osbert looked so regal when he made this pronouncement that I expected him to be in the gold lace and ample cloak of an eighteenth-century general concerned about the winter rot that had set in among his officers. "It is time for the arts to assert themselves."

"Not on our rations." I reflected gloomily about the soggy lump of bread that we had tried to toast that morning. It was otherwise inedible. "One way to keep the population quiet is to starve it." Then I felt that lifting of the spirit that comes only with recognition after days of being ignored and we spent the next hour discussing the hall, it had already been booked, the probable program and the convenience of the date.

I also had my task and my reward. Edith arrived at Lowndes a few days later to time Hilda's reading. She brought with her a poem she had just written and asked me to type her out a few copies. It was *Heart and Mind*, the poem I like most of all her work, a major lyric of the English language and one that brings back to me the courage of those wartime days whenever I read it. It speaks both of the conflict of the artist and the one from which no human being can escape although it is possibly the artist who is most sensitive to it: the struggle between human feelings and abstract truth, the final battle between perception and intellect.

My early life had trained me to be a servitor of the arts. Osbert, Edith and H.D. were in many ways too sensitive. There had to be a shield and I was tough. If I had bothered about what people thought of me when I was young I should never have survived. So, that afternoon, as I had copied out the poem, I felt it was a little chaplet thrown to me by the gods. I have never understood why the impact of greatness is supposed to be calm. It is like the sudden eruption of a volcano. It touches something beyond consciousness on the other side of the mind until there is, for a moment, a sense of suffocation.

Edith and Hilda were among the rare writers who could read their own poetry. Edith knew the precise value of every word and exactly how it should be spoken. She told me that she had trained herself by working with an actress from the Comédie Française while she had lived in Paris. "I knew how English poetry ought to be read," she once told me, "but not at first the technique of its delivery. I felt it was wiser to learn this in a foreign language and in that way afterwards I could develop my own style."

Hilda read magnificently like the inspired muse she was, not only her own poems but those by other writers. Only she and Edith have spoken the sounds that, as I say, "echo in the inside of the ear." Edith had the technique, the control and a complete mastery of her audience,

Hilda the inspiration and the fire so that she was to me and many of her listeners the seer prophesying from the steps of a Greek temple above a brilliant sea. I have heard many people read during my life but none with the power that Hilda and Edith had at their peak, a sensation that the sound was right, the color of the words balanced and the listener carried into a different world that for me was as outer space.

April 14th. The Day at last arrived. It was memorable for me because for the first and I trust the only time in my life, I jumped on to a moving taxi. They were hard to find and how was I to get Hilda to the Aeolian Hall and the reading otherwise? It was too far for her to walk. She had had the eight coupons necessary for a new black dress and it had been made for her by the late Queen Mary's dressmaker, who happened to be a friend of mine; so as far as clothes went, all was correct. One male poet, told he had to appear in a stiff collar, found he had none and that his wife had used up all his coupons. Another man had totally disappeared. Still a third was reported to have rehearsed his offering to his wife for hours in bed. The slogan was in general, "Of course I'm not nervous, why should I be? It is such an opportunity to hear how one's verses sound." There had been endless telephone calls, "Tell Hilda we peck three times and die once" had been one mysterious message. I presumed it was a reference to curtsies. No singers ever displayed more temperament, the males being far more flamboyant than the females.

An organ had been draped with tapestries, chairs were arranged in a half circle on the platform, Kenneth Maggs had lent a large lectern for the occasion. I had selected some seats near the aisle so that I could move rapidly to Hilda's rescue if necessary. Robert was one side of me. Faith the other. We bowed solemnly to Ivy Compton-Burnett and Margaret Jourdain who were sitting a row or two away. Beatrice Lillie was selling programs, a group of gentlemen gathered unobtrusively by the entrance. People stopped talking. I heard Osbert say, "Shall I lead?" and the Queen entered followed by the two Princesses. I fixed my eyes in the best boarding-school tradition, "never stare," on the back of the chair in front of me and by the time I judged it correct to look up, the poets had been led to their places. They were going to enjoy themselves once their ordeal was over but for the time being most of them looked agitated or unhappy.

The Reading was to be in alphabetical order. This was a wise precaution. It was to have begun with Binyon but he had died a day or so previously, so first a poem was read in his memory. Blunden and Gordon Bottomley followed. Bottomley was a huge, cheerful man who enjoyed his declamation and took me back to the days when I had seen his name in some of the "little magazines."

Hilda was third. She looked like one of the Muses and like them, she was speaking of the eternal conflict between wisdom and the world. I had not heard the poem before but as I listened my mind went back to the days when I had first discovered *Sea Garden* and murmured lines from it constantly as I walked in winter beside the cold, gray English waves. Then, merging as pictures sometimes do in our minds, more swiftly and more full of the original emotion than any film can recall, I was myself knocking at a door in Cornwall and looking up for the first time at the Ionic face that was already so familiar from statues seen in the South. Then again, how swiftly our impressions dissolve and reappear, I was sitting beside her on the slopes above Sunion and looking down at a Greek sea that was the color of her eyes.

Now instead of sunshine or the colorful London of her youth where Hilda had first met so many of the people Osbert had gathered for the Reading, she was speaking to us of the inner wisdom without which creation is impossible, and remembering those

> who when the earth-quake shook their city,
> when angry blast and fire
>
> broke open their frail door,
> did not forget
> beauty.

It was H.D. who expressed more than any other writer the deeply felt but perhaps not always conscious feelings of the Londoners during the war.

Eliot followed, it was only inappropriate that he should have ended with "London Bridge is falling down" because whatever else London was doing at that moment, it was a growling, enraged lion with a "no surrender" air firmly about its whiskers. Walter de la Mare then read

The Listeners and the first half of the program ended with John Masefield.

I had always longed to meet Masefield but I had to wait for this till the war was over; then I was introduced in person to the famous ducks. At least on this particular afternoon, I saw him. He has never been properly understood as a writer. The Victorian giants were dead by the time he began his work but his poverty cut him off from the new and exciting experiments that were then beginning in London. His best work is the least known. It would be hard to find a better account of a boy's adolescence at the turn of the century than his *New Chum*. His *In the Mill* is as excellent a record of a young man's struggle to become an author in spite of isolation, little money and exile. I pass sometimes near the American countryside where he lived and worked for a couple of years and I am always astonished that he crammed more into that book than travelers often record in volumes three times its length. He saw America with young eyes and no fixed opinions and thus recorded the cold and the color, the harshness of some of his fellow workers and the kindness of others, as if it were the first time that such events and such emotions had ever been written down. I liked some of his early poems and sea stories. These have been spoilt for many because they are considered "safe" reading for schools and so later they evoke only unpleasant memories of boredom and battered desks. I read them where they were meant to be read, tossing about in a small boat off a windy, dangerous coast. His lack of funds, his age, he was caught between two traditions and generations, cut him off from our complete overthrow of conventional forms. Oxford was the refuge that had offered him peace after the grim conditions he had had to face for years and I know that he helped old and young in every possible way for the rest of his life. Few of them remembered his assistance afterwards. The word for him was gentleness. I am proud that though for geographical reasons we could not often meet, we corresponded after I got back to Burier and I treasure some enchanting letters from him. At the Reading, however, because of his ducks, I had to be content with Hilda's report that he had been very, very kind.

An interval was announced. We all stood up, again with eyes fixed decorously on the ground, everybody pretending with complete nonsuccess that it was an ordinary occasion while flashlights flashed, cameras clicked, and the procession left again in the complete tradition of a Jacobean Court with Osbert leading firmly as Master of the Revels. The poets, I heard later, were taken off to another room, one male poet remarking sadly that he had never expected to feel like the member of a football team being lined up to be presented before the Cup Final. We, ourselves, felt this to be ill-timed levity.

The British Council had asked me to look after the Chinese representative during the pause. Why, I could not guess until it occurred to me that they had probably mixed it up with Persia. I struggled dutifully over to the other side of the hall to greet the representative. We bowed, neither of us could think of anything to say, fortunately he noticed a friend coming towards him. We bowed once more and I scurried back to my seat. On the way I had the good fortune to hear a girl in uniform murmur, "Rather lovely, I thought, the last woman's poem." "Did you, my dear," her dowager escort answered, "but we don't know who *she* is." I knew Hilda would appreciate that story.

I sat down again in the middle of much anxiety. A lady poet (better nameless) was so much overcome by the occasion that she had sipped rather too much cordial to appease her nerves. Various gentlemen were making efforts to persuade her to retire but instead she turned on one (so elderly, so respectable) and thinking it was Osbert, began to whack him heartily with her stick. I watched entranced, knowing that I was unlikely to be involved. People lost their heads, nobody knew what to do until Beatrice Lillie, dropping her programs, took control and led the lady firmly from the aisle just before the solemn return of the regal procession. It was so like a sketch that Robert and I had just seen her do on the stage that in spite of the occasion, I was helpless with laughter. "Try to control yourself," Robert whispered angrily, "or they will think you are in the same condition." I have never been able to decide whether a sense of humor is a gift from the gods or one of life's greater discomforts.

Vita Sackville-West opened the second part of the program. She read easily and well although the poem was perhaps a little long. On such occasions it is hard to hold the concentration of the audience. Then, to my delight,

Edith stepped forward as if from some great tapestry to give us *Anne Boleyn's Song* as only she could read it and at that moment it became not only a poem of memory and loss but also of the rise and fall of an epoch that exactly fitted the times. Renishaw came into the mind as she was reciting it and the long, lonely nights she had spent there thinking about her friends in Paris from whom she had had no news and of what was happening to creative work in all parts of the world. It was often easier to be deeply involved as we all were in London than to have to watch a great catastrophe from its edge. I had only to think of my own survival and my friends; Edith felt the burden of humanity as a whole.

Then it was Osbert's turn. His first poem was an eighteenth-century elegy and then he brought us back to earth with a few gay rhymes about a carpenter. Once more we were in a world of Masques. Afterwards, alas, we had a debacle. Our next poet sprang to the lectern and stayed there. It was his moment, he was going to make it last. He was timed to finish at a certain moment. Did he care? Certainly not. He read and read, it appeared to be about colts in a field and dreams but the words flowed on in an intense mumble that few of us could comprehend. People coughed. He took no notice. Finally even he had to pause a second for breath. Then his fellow poets rose as one, applauding him but forcing him back unwillingly into his seat. It was sad, however, because it left Arthur Waley only time for a single poem and we all, including it was rumored our royal visitors, liked and admired his work.

At the finish we rose again and were decorous; all, I fear, except our dear Mrs. Ash. "Madam," she said to me the next morning, "I thought it might be the only chance I ever had of seeing them so when Mr. Waley started I slipped out to the barrier and I saw the Queen, as near to me as you are yourself. Oh, it was beautiful, beautiful, I never enjoyed an afternoon so much in my life."

People began to file out, so as soon as possible I tried to get to Hilda but charging as I often do with my head in a battering-ram position, I all but knocked one of the more august poets over. I found Hilda most *émue* over the Princesses. They had worn mittens. (I could not imagine why that should provoke such emotion but it did!) I reminded her that it was fortunate that it had been an English and not a Persian affair. In Persia, as I carefully explained, she would have had to crawl across a carpet on her hands and knees to be presented, banging her forehead nine times on the floor and then she would have had to address the "pardishah" in the first person singular pronoun and the third person plural verb, a grammatical form said to indicate omnipotence. (Where I had acquired this odd information myself, I cannot now remember.) Instead, as she had apparently done her three curtsies correctly, I led her home, actually getting another taxi, to tea and a full discussion of the afternoon.

The excitements of the day were not yet over, however. Early that evening the telephone rang and when I answered it, a voice asked for Hilda. "Who is it?" I inquired, fearing a strayed and starving poet looking for shelter.

"It's Norman Pearson."

I was puzzled for a moment because we had had letters from him recently from America. "Oh, what a pity! You missed the Poets' Reading this afternoon. Hilda got presented to the Queen." This was all I had time to say before H.D. snatched the receiver from me. It seemed strange for him to ring up precisely at this moment because as he was (and is) a historian of the arts, he would have enjoyed the historical significance of the afternoon more than any of us.

The call was also to mean a great deal to me although I did not know it at the time. It was Norman who was responsible for much of my own subsequent work. It would be helpful to know the method he applied: intuition or a form of analysis practiced by somebody I respected as a tough and passionate fighter. He forced me back to my earliest beginnings; when I said I was interested in Greenland, I was not offered books but found myself instead looking down at the carcass of a recently shot polar bear. He saw that I could write inwards from actual experience but not outwards from just imagination. Whatever I have done has emerged from mutual kicks, snarls, or the sudden production of an unexpected adventure at precisely the right moment. It must not be supposed that I am grateful in any conventional sense. Nobody enjoys being sent up to the masthead to contemplate past errors. But Norman knew and applied the only treatment that would work with me when it came to producing books.

All this happened after the war but that telephone call was the beginning of our friendship. It proved how right I was to say at the beginning, "It is only in America that I shall find myself."

A few days after the Reading, Edith gave one of her big tea parties. The assembly was not important, it was the gathering of us together that mattered. I had the privilege of seeing Edith alone in her room so that it was understood between us that on such occasions I should not come to the circle round her but should take the first vacant chair in the ring beyond. I never knew who my companion would be, a painter, an actor, some friend from her early days in London, come up from the country for a day. We usually managed to talk together as if we were intimate friends, knowing that we should probably not meet again. On one occasion I took the first seat I could find and was immediately greeted by my neighbor. It was Sylva Norman and I cannot remember which of us first said "Queenwood." I do not think we had met since I had dropped my straw hat with the eaglet band round it into the bottom of a cupboard, but from the moment I had read her delightful novel, *Nature Has No Tune*, we had corresponded. Why has that book never been reprinted? Our meeting hardly seemed real at first but we were soon talking as if we had never been separated. It was odd to think that we had once stood in line in a drafty school hall and should never have met again until invited by Edith to her party. I am afraid that afternoon our early memories effaced our immediate surroundings. Two segments of my own life seemed to come together as in a puzzle, memories of my school days and the writing world into which, with Hilda's help, I had ultimately fought my way.

Edith had had no idea that we knew each other and was most amused when I told her about the meeting. Yet many people found old friends or made new ones at her parties. It was an attempt to give us some cohesion at a time when "directives" had scattered people all over England. I heard the actors of the day discuss Shakespeare with her and musicians music they were composing, that after the war became world-known. There were also people with a love for poetry who could not themselves create it. We may not always have come away with ideas but we did walk out into the battered streets with a little hope. Surely that was an achievement in what I called the "terrible years" when no ending seemed possible.

I can only record a deeply felt love and gratitude to both Edith and Osbert. The arts owed them much and their loyalty should be remembered.

Life in wartime was a mixture of waiting and frustration to which was added once a year the battle of the ration books. We listened to our instructions on the radio more intently than we did for bombs, we stood in rows for hours to get the new issue and watched our neighbors on the buses so as to leap out if possible in front of them. We tried to wriggle our way to the head of the queue but even so, it meant the loss of a whole morning.

The opposite side of Lowndes Square was in Westminster but our block was in Chelsea; it was then a friendly, almost country village. We lined up along a street just off the King's Road in front of the Food Office and those of us who were lucky enough to get a place towards the entrance faced a large sign that said *Prams*. There we stuck, a lump of ammonites halfway up a cliff but holding in the process, as I muttered, "The lights of Europe." Where was Sylvia? Where was Adrienne? I had heard nothing of them since June 1940, when a letter had reached me posted just before the Germans entered Paris. "Don't worry about us," Sylvia had written, "it's only the time between one holiday and the next, we shall soon be together again." It was three years since then, three years and eleven days to be exact.

"It opens at nine, doesn't it?" My neighbor's face had the yellow tinge that came from both the blackout and our badly planned diet. The violets on my neighbor's toque, she must have dug it out of an attic because they had not been fashionable since I was seven, made her face look even more sallow than it was. Otherwise she was wearing what had become our summer uniform, a sedate dress of broad blue and white stripes that had really been intended for dust sheets but which the wise now hunted from shop to shop because of its indestructible quality. "Or is it," she looked round anxiously, "nine thirty?"

"It's nine but they're never punctual."

"Do you know if Milks are in the same room as Emergencies?" Somebody behind us seemed very worried.

"Will they give me my mother-in-law's book or must she fetch it herself?"

The inquiries passing up and down the line gave it a semblance of life, otherwise we had regressed into some infantile state without even the solace of grumbling aloud.

> Sleep in a cave
> if you want to be happy,
> save your dog's hair
> if you want to keep warm.

If I muttered some such doggerel to my neighbor's artificial violets as a protest against Whitehall's determination to flatten the British soul, would she look surprised or turn on me with indignation? Yet we were nearer the Pleistocene age than peace. I was trying to work out how I would have organized the distribution myself when my neighbor shoved me, and the queue, obeying some mysterious inner signal because the Food Office was still shut, began to move up the path.

There was a rattle of bolts. The doors slowly opened. We moved into a dignified scrum to push into a parlor and face a large poster begging us to "Dig for Victory." How stupid could Whitehall be? First they preached economy. Then they urged us to waste precious seeds in London's polluted soil. A clerk chewed the top of her Utility pencil, looked at her face carefully in a pocket mirror, replaced the glass in her handbag and put this into a drawer. Then, and only then, she deigned to glance at us. "First, please," she snapped.

By the time I got out, clasping the two books for Hilda

and myself, the queue stretched far down the King's Road.

Some weeks later I had to visit the Food Office again to get a temporary card as I was going for a week to Eckington. It was still crowded although I had to go to another department.

"I've come about my ration book again," a flustered female in a hat covered with overblown roses (Edwardian perhaps, we had all ransacked our attics and the early twentieth century ran to flowers) broke the queue to our astonishment and pushed to the front.

I was thankful that I had a notebook with me and apart from the address I took the conversation down precisely as I heard it. I doubt if an author could invent it.

"I'm afraid we have no news of it, madam."

"But I gave the form in weeks ago and the book has never arrived."

"Our records show that it was posted to you at ten, Middlesex Terrace."

"It never reached me."

"Of course, if you are not there . . ."

"*There!*" Hat, roses and the table shook as the woman thumped it in indignation. "*There!* But I am there. It's my home. I've lived there for twenty years."

"You told me last week that you had left that address."

"I told you, last week, Miss," the tone was witheringly sarcastic, "that I had been at home every time the postman called except one Saturday when I had gone to stay a night with my niece who has just had her first baby but

I got back on the Sunday. I haven't been away for years."

"You will have to inquire at the Post Office."

"But I have inquired!" The picture hat swept round to include us all in the splendor of her accusation. "I came here three . . . weeks . . . ago," she thumped the table at every word, "and I reported that I had never received my book. You sent me to our local post office, they sent me to the central office for the district and they sent me back to my own home to starve. I have been to every post office for miles."

"Nice that you had the time," somebody commented from the back row. It was hard to judge whether she was being sympathetic or bitter.

"I *haven't* the time. Who do you think I am?" Roses swung round again to face us all indignantly.

"Sorry, madam, you will have to wait. I have no instructions."

"How do I eat?" It was a howl of rage from the heart.

"Sorry, madam, I have no instructions. Come back in a week if it doesn't turn up. Next, please." This time it was not a suggestion but a command.

"I've come about my diabetes card," the woman next in the queue almost whispered, "it said on the B.B.C. last night it was time to fetch them."

"The B.B.C. is not the Food Office. Have you got your medical certificate?"

"Yes, here," the woman offered it eagerly.

"I am sorry, madam, but you will have to come again. We have no instructions."

"Oh, dear," the woman was almost in tears, "it's such a long way and my husband's ill as well."

"Sorry. Come again in four days. Next, please."

"A week's Emergency, please. I have to go north on business." I handed over my ration book.

An Emergency was routine. "I see you have had your tea, dear," she stamped a card and handed it and the book back to me. "Next, please." A woman began a story about a niece having come to live with her, and a steady trickle of newcomers pushed through the door as I went out.

It is possible that something was wrong with the first woman's story although it was only too probable that the book had been stolen. They fetched a good price on the black market. There was no reason, however, to drag suffering people like the second applicant twice over for the trivial amount of invalid diet allotted. "Useless mouths," one official had said to me about similar cases; "in times like these, if people can't work for the war effort, why should we keep them alive?" He was in a Government job with a warm suit on his back and I hated him and the Appeasers of all ranks who had got us into the mess as much as I hated the enemy. There was courage, endurance and infinite kindness among all ranks in wartime London but there was robbery and cruelty as well, as there always is, in peace as well as war.

All we are given is a string of moments, everything else we lose. Some of mine came during the war in Aldermanbury and Cripplegate. They began when Gerald Henderson invited me to go for a walk with him one Sunday round old London.

Few people can have known more about the City than Gerald. He was a librarian at St. Paul's, a student of its archives and a member of its famous wartime Watch. His wife, Cole, an artist, was a friend of Hilda's and had known my mother well till she had died and both Gerald and Cole had been members of our Lowndes Group from the start.

We met each other at a bus stop near the cathedral and as we started out across the dunes of gritty dust, Gerald paused now and then beside some ruin to tell me its history from medieval times to its destruction during the great City raids. Each stone to him was some archaic jewel that could never be replaced. People had died there but as the City was not a place where many slept, the holocaust of the big attacks had been further away and where is there a street in any town that has not seen death? At present it was a wilderness of flowers. A warden told me later that he had counted over fifty varieties but I remember most the daisies nested in the cracks, pink campion, huge masses of the purple willow herb and a tiny blue flower that must have sprung from seed blown there from a country lane. They made gardens of a still standing wall, they crept along the gash in an old tile, they shot up between the cracks of a broken floor. All of them edged this vast empire without a name, this new myth on the border of consciousness where death and sorrow were remote. I was so lost inside this curious enchantment that I hardly noticed what Gerald was saying to me till I caught the word "Agincourt."

"What?" I stopped beside a bit of undamaged wall, ashamed that I had not been paying more attention to him.

"I begged the authorities to remove them."

I must have looked puzzled because Gerald added hastily, "The bells."

"Bells? Agincourt?"

"The bells were still hanging here that were rung to announce the victory."

"Agincourt!" It still seemed terribly far away.

"There was no direct hit. Look, most of the church is still standing but the flames burnt through the ropes. The bells dropped and were smashed."

"But why didn't they move them at the beginning of the war?"

"They didn't care."

"The bells of Agincourt." Was it a presage of the doom of Britain? I think now more than ever that it was. It was the same indifference that led to Munich and to omitting to use in full the year that we had so shamefully won. A nation is rootless that neglects its own past and that medieval battle had its lesson for us. It was won by initiative and the use of new weapons, the bows of the highly trained English archers, against a French army that had not changed its habits of thought for years.

I can see us now as in an endless dream, walking across the wilderness where tiles and daisies in mosaic fragments touched each other among the shattered stones.

In spite of the sunlight it seemed a cold and terrifying day. "Perhaps," Gerald suggested, "the dust on our shoes is from the bells."

There are moments when destiny puts the right book into the hands of an apprentice. I discovered, prowling among the books in my father's library when I was fifteen, Hazlitt's *The Dramatic Literature of the Age of Elizabeth*. It was there that I found Bellario, Philaster's page. Nobody had told me that a girl's part on the Elizabethan stage had been played by a boy. I learned her speeches and quoted them to myself during the stresses of school. I had forgotten about her for years until "sniffing" along the shelves in the London Library I found T. W. Baldwin's *The Organisation and Personnel of the Shakespearean Company*. I took it out by chance and carried it back to read (I hoped undisturbed by bombs) peacefully during the evenings. I made some notes but I was not particularly excited until I came almost to the end of the book. Then it was literally as if the thunderbolt of Zeus had struck me. Baldwin was attempting to assign to members of the company the different parts that each one might have acted, and suggested that Bellario might have been played by James Sands.

Why should such a discovery have meant so much to me? Our present was full of raids and hardships, our future was uncertain. Perhaps it was because of a gift I sometimes have of seeing not the "exterior case" as the Elizabethans would say, but a flash, an intuition, of the interior mind. I grew up among the frustrations and tragedies of the First World War, they were far worse than the second, and what youth was I never knew. Bellario may have been unconsciously a symbol to me of what I felt I had lost.

People say I have an Elizabethan ear. It would be surprising if it were otherwise. Twice, each time during a war, I have dreamed, read and almost slept with the language ringing in my ears, to a point I have thought its thoughts. Afterwards it drops away, so little remembered that to my shame I cannot even recall some of the main dates of the age if asked a sudden question. Yet in a crisis, it is often with me again, distinct from the present day, as full of fears as it is of colors but felt as an actual experience, it has no dreamlike quality about it.

My next expedition was to Silver Street. I wanted to find the site of Shakespeare's house because thanks to the researches of Professor and Mrs. C. W. Wallace at the Court of Requests, it is known that Shakespeare lived there for several years. Mountjoy or Montjoie was a Huguenot tire or headdress maker and Shakespeare was called as a witness in a suit that concerned Stephen Bellot, an apprentice. Bellot had married his master's daughter and that had led to the commonest of Elizabethan lawsuits, a dispute over her dowry.

Most English people continue to believe that "we know nothing about Shakespeare as a person." Actually we know a great deal. One reason for their ignorance is that the information is often contained in rather abstruse books that only the specialist is likely to read, and another is the setting of some of the plays for examinations.

They are then ruined for ever. I should never have read the Elizabethans for pleasure as I have done all my life if I had heard of them first in a classroom. Yet their world was very different from our own, and what is needed in a school is a general course on the customs of that time, a survey of the manner in which its values differed from those of today, the main historical events and the way people of all classes lived. How many realize, for instance, that a man could not travel from his market town to London, unless he were a nobleman or a wealthy landowner, without a paper that was virtually a passport?

I wandered up and down Aldermanbury but the devastation was so great that I should never have found Silver Street if a policeman had not directed me to the ruins. Even then I should have missed the actual site except for an incident that the Elizabethans would have appreciated. I knew that in recent times a public house had stood there, and now, to comply with the licensing regulations, a board had been put up stating that the tavern would be rebuilt directly after the war. At least I could look down upon the fire-blackened stones and know that I was near the place where Shakespeare had probably written some of his greatest plays. He would have understood the Blitz and the courage of his Londoners while deploring the prewar foolishness of their rulers.

There is a limit to the amount of time one can stare at a few stones. I bowed solemnly to the inn sign and walked off towards Cripplegate.

Twenty years after the war I could not even find the

place. It was apparently under some of the most hideous buildings I have ever seen, without even a plaque to mark the site. I think it would have been a tribute both to Shakespeare and the heroic fire fighters of the area if that small corner had been converted into a national monument.

Nobody now can see Aldermanbury as it once was, a sea of flowers in a city of desolation. It may seem strange to write this about the wreckage left by bombs and fire but the area between St. Mary's Church and the cathedral in that summer of 1943 was one of the most beautiful places I have seen. Yet I knew many of the great landscapes of the world, the Alps in their summer and their winter glory, the wide, tawny desert, the curving Mediterranean bays. All these were a part of memory but this suddenly quiet island rising from an avalanche of ruins was their equal. The stones had tumbled from the walls exactly as they had at Paestum but their dusty surface was a blaze of color. Here was a clump of marigolds, there was some viper's bugloss, but it was the willow herb that had taken possession of the place, spreading its purple banner across the dust. All was silence but it was sunny and as far as this could be a consolation, in that time of frustration and unhappiness, if all the other virtues were in retreat, beauty stayed.

St. Mary's itself was an empty shell. Sometimes I wandered round it, looking up at the tufts of grass that clung to the cracks along the wall. It was hard to imagine the Elizabethan congregation that had gathered there on

Sundays, just as afraid of the plague as we were now of bombs, but this was the parish church of Heminge and Condell, the two men who preserved seventeen (some authorities say eighteen) of Shakespeare's plays for us for which no Quartos are known to exist. Many of our favorite quotations would have perished without them. Both had been married at the church, their children had been buried there and Heminge had remembered Aldermanbury in his will, "where I have long lived and whither I have bequeathed my body for burial." He had moved late in life for some reason, possibly after the death of his wife, to the Bankside. Once when I was wandering down the street a man came up to me, probably a warden off duty, and asked me if I were looking for something?

"Yes, for the houses that belonged to Heminge and Condell." He was obviously from the neighborhood but I doubted if he would recognize the names.

"Oh, the Folio chaps. Have you got the numbers of their houses?"

"My references say that possibly, but only possibly, they lived at 69 and 74."

"Then you're too far from the church."

As they say, the English are unpredictable. It gives us a bad reputation on the Continent. My friends had already warned me, "If you keep poking your nose into those rubbish heaps, you'll get arrested as a spy." Yet here was a man with a profound knowledge of his neighborhood though less, I suspected, of Elizabethan days who was prepared to give up a portion of his off-duty afternoon to helping a complete stranger trace the site of an Elizabethan house. We walked on for a few paces and then he pointed to a white tiled space that had probably been a washroom, lying as if it had been scrubbed that morning between low, broken walls. "That would have been about the place," he remarked. Only the foundations were left, open to the sky, with purple flowers covering what had once been offices. The Elizabethan houses would have disappeared centuries before and the ruins were Victorian but it was still the ground where Shakespeare's friends had talked and argued with him or listened for St. Mary's bell on Sundays.

"Are you sure that your identification of the numbers is correct?" The warden seemed as interested as I was in my search.

"We can never be certain but they lived here according to the records and most authorities agree that these are the probable numbers."

"I should like to know more about them." He seemed disappointed that I could tell him so little of their lives except that Heminge was a church warden but we agreed that a walk on Sunday rested the mind and that it was lucky the last months had been so quiet.

"Dreadful night it was, the night of the Fire." He looked across the waste ground with the terrible, uncomplaining look of London's citizens. It was not only their property that they had lost but much of their history as well. I had watched their faces turn from surprise to resignation and I was to see them change once more to bitter anger in 1945.

It was time to go home. I promised to let the warden

know if I found out any more about "the Folio chaps"
but following his directions as to a quick way back to the
bus stop, I turned a corner and found myself in front of a
tiny island, green, undisturbed, floating, it seemed,
among the ruins. There were benches round a bust of
Shakespeare that had been put up in 1896 with an in-
scription to the memory of Heminge and Condell for
their work in bringing out the Folio. On that particular
Sunday afternoon several old men and two young women
were sitting sleepily round it in the sun, thinking, I suspected, the most modern of thoughts. (Would they get a
box of matches at the grocer's or would he be "out"
again, could they stretch the tea ration to the end of the
month?) I looked at the head, it was *kitsch* but for that
reason it was one of us, it did not have to be stored in the
country or muffled up with sacks, and I thought of
Shakespeare's two friends who had forgotten their own
ambitions to save every line they could of his work. Comradeship, always a form of love, counts at the end. The
moment was one of the closest affiliations with the Elizabethan age that I have ever felt and was over in a flash;
because of its intensity it could not last.

Aldermanbury! A symbol of a city, of resistance, even
of the struggle to retain a fragment of eternity. Perhaps a
knot of sixteenth-century dust rubbed off on me as I went
home to weak tea, soggy bread and marge.

I saw Faith from time to time and we should have met
more frequently had it not been almost as difficult to get
to Hampstead in wartime as it was to Derbyshire. Some-

times in the summer when the trains were less crowded, I
went out to dinner with her. I was there in July when the
landings in Sicily had begun and she was happy at the
thought that one day she might return to Capri again. It
was on that particular evening that I met Nicolas Nadejine for the first time, a Russian who towered above me
as the mountains tower over Lake Leman and a man with
one of the strangest personal stories that I have ever
heard.

Nadejine belonged to a middle-class family in a big
Russian city and aged about sixteen saw a crowd on his
way to school. Like any boy, he had strolled over to see
what was happening and had been promptly arrested!
This part of his story can only be appreciated by those
who knew him because he was the most nonpolitical
being one could meet. What he had was a talent for getting into impossible situations that sometimes proved
highly favorable and were at others really tragic.

He was sent to Siberia but on arrival he was met by a
man who had received money from Nadejine's family to
help him get away. "Escape!" (You should have heard
him tell the story!) "Escape! With all this hunting? Certainly not." So he had joined a trapper for a couple of
years until he got bored with the life and the intense
cold. Then he collected the funds that his family had sent
him and returned to Europe by ship. It must have been
around 1910.

He settled on Capri where the Compton Mackenzies
had taken an interest in him and as he had a good voice,
had helped him to study singing. It was supposed that he

would stay on the island for life as there was already a group of Russian exiles there. To everyone's amusement, he announced that he "smelt war in the air" and almost without funds, went off to England. Life at first was difficult but in 1914 he got a job at a Government office translating Russian documents and was rewarded by being granted British nationality of which he was very proud, once the conflict was over. He returned to Capri shortly afterwards and resumed his friendship with the Mackenzies. Occasionally he wandered away, once to sing with an opera company in the Fiji Islands, but as soon as his funds were replenished, he went back to Italy. Again he had smelt something in the air and by the outbreak of the war he was in London once more and at his old job of translating documents as if there had been no break between 1914 and 1939.

He wrote his autobiography in English but neglected to finish the final chapters. He gave me the manuscript before he died but because it had no ending we were unable to find a publisher for it. He also wrote poems in Russian that I could not read. Friends have told me that they are traditional and rather old-fashioned. By 1943 he had appointed himself Faith's guardian and he looked after her in an impersonal way, with some interludes, until shortly before she died. I mistrust romantic stories about exile as a rule but in Nadejine's case whatever I was able to check was true. His manuscript is full of rich moments and unfinished endings, more like a film than a book, and full of turn-of-the-century adventures that seem remote and improbable today. Now even the memory that lives could be lived in such a manner is being lost.

That evening however was an exiles' meeting. Some of us are citizens not of a country but a landscape; with Faith it was Capri, with myself, Burier. If the landings in Sicily were successful, they might open the way for us to go home. You cannot turn back the years as if they were the pages of a book, all beauty has a time of growth and flowering that eventually must perish and each day that passed represented a sunrise, the light falling on a favorite tree, a particular mood that we had lost. Yet it was extraordinary that evening how much happier we felt for even a little hope.

It was also a moment of lost contacts suddenly renewed. On my return to Lowndes I was coming out of the Knightsbridge Underground when a voice greeted me and I saw my cousin John for the first time in a year. He was in the army and I knew that his duties kept him out of London. We seldom wrote to each other but with our craving for independence and adventure we were more alike than the rest of the family. I was grateful to him for accepting the fact that I had preferred to live abroad. We stood on the corner for a few minutes exchanging news, he was not cheerful, "It will be another three years" but at least he added that Switzerland would be waiting for me when I could return. Why is it that a chance meeting persists in memory while the longer holidays we had spent together in childhood are forgotten?

I knew from the moment that I saw Cornwall that it was my country; I was, I think, about ten. I also knew by some strange intuition that I should be unlikely to live there. My mother found it desolate, my father was lukewarm so that it was not until I went to boarding school that my first real contact began. By chance I sat next to Doris who was half-Scillonian and half-Cornish and a year later her parents invited me to go with her and her sister, Ethel, for a few days to the islands during our summer holidays.

It was an instantaneous falling in love. What had I ever wanted more of a country than sea, islands and boats? In those far-off days as we crossed over on the *Lyonnesse,* we could land on any uninhabited islet we wished and rule it for a day. We bathed, picked up shells, cowries were the great prize, scrambled about among the bracken and heather or occasionally went out in a small boat to fish. The English (that different race as we said scornfully) were hardly aware that our islands existed. Now because the fish have become scarce and the early daffodils that fill the fields are at the mercy of storms, we who are old Scillonians accept the fact that tourists have to be encouraged if the islanders are to earn a living but naturally, in our hearts, we regret the days when even to see a puffin on the rocks near where we were sitting seemed an intrusion. More than anything I value an old fisherman's remark to me during a recent visit. "You've been around here a long time, haven't you?" I have, I have been going there since 1911.

110

During the war nobody was allowed to cross to the Scillies unless their families were living there. It was a necessary security measure. Doris, however, had settled down some years earlier on a bulb farm near St. Keverne and she invited me down every summer for a brief respite from Lowndes. We were not allowed to go on the sands because of barbed wire, many of the cliff paths were barred, but it was Cornwall, we could walk freely along the lanes where the banks were a flower garden because there was no one to cut the foxgloves back and we were seeing the land, I suppose, as it might have been in the eighteenth century. We seldom heard a plane and while the rationing was strict, being a district of farms the quality was excellent and at times, because of restricted transport, there was even a little extra. In actuality as well as in my mind I was living in two worlds, battered streets and craters for much of the year and then a few weeks in the salt air far from the charred smells of London.

In 1943 I could not get away before the beginning of August. I usually took the night train because there was more chance of getting a seat. I went to Paddington an hour ahead of time and luckily found a pleasant girl porter who took my case and led me to the end of the platform where the train was supposed to arrive. "Whatever you do, dear," she warned me, "don't leave your bag for an instant." In those days of coupons, second-hand clothes were fetching a high price.

"I suppose the crowds have been awful," I said, wishing that the journey were over. "Well, yes," she straightened her porter's cap, "but I don't mind the people so much, it's the rabbits."

"The what?"

"The rabbits, dear. This year people are taking their rabbits with them, I had my barrow full of them last week."

Naturally at that moment rabbits were more valuable than jewels and unless somebody in the family stayed at home who was going to feed and guard them? It was another sign of the times, people mistrusted their neighbors and the animals, being a potential source of food, were apt to be stolen.

"We live in a time of difficulties," I murmured; then I sat down precariously on my suitcase and tried to immerse myself in a pocket edition of Beaumont and Fletcher, as a reminder that travel in Elizabethan days was more uncomfortable and hazardous than a train trip in wartime England.

I got a seat and slept most of the way to Plymouth when a guard woke us and said we had to move along to the front of the train. After we got out and rushed up the platform we found the door to the front coach was still locked. We were inventive in those days, a soldier leaned out of the window and grabbed my case, then two others took me by the arms and pulled. A final heave and I found myself upon the knees of a fourth to shouts of "Half-Time, bring up the oranges" or "Throw Out the Life Line," this last from a hymn. Another woman and myself were jammed into the corridor beside the four soldiers and stood, literally shoulder to shoulder, till we got to the next station. The woman, she was nearest to the window, had the temerity to remark, "Have you ever seen anywhere as lovely as England?" I was somewhat bad-tempered by that time and yelled back, "Yes, New York, and I wish I were there." At Truro, where I had to change, however, I got a corner seat in the little train that connected it in those days with Helston, opposite a large colonel who helped me with my luggage. He was looking forward to his leave as much as I was to my holiday and observed, "I've got a granite pillbox near Land's End." During our subsequent conversation I found out that he meant a cottage.

Yet there was something about Cornwall that made us forget the difficulties of getting there. It was older, less tolerant of the human race yet offering some sudden moment of illumination such as I have never felt in any other land. Once there, I never wanted to leave it yet I also knew that I should do no work, moment would succeed moment of hibernation and dream. Only those who have been actually born there know the antidote and can carry out the usual tasks of life. I had the strange feeling that though I was perfectly conscious of what was going on around me, I was also living somewhere else, except that words are too hard of outline to describe the actual sensation. The feeling as with many dreams was blurred.

We were not apart from the war in Cornwall but it was a different war. The cottage folk watched the weather because their sons were at sea. Life was hidden by the mist that blew in suddenly on a clear afternoon as well as by the lack of news. I sometimes felt that living so near to shoals and rocks the people were both more aware and more resigned than we were in London but this may have been imagination. Then I would stare at the blue veronica dividing a path from the neighboring kitchen garden and wonder if they knew what London had had to endure? It is natural to think that one's own particular danger is worse. I was already thinking about *The Fourteenth of October* though I did not write the book till later, but wherever I wandered a sense of doom or resignation or revolt seemed round me in the cottages and lanes. The people who dig the fields, the men who sail the fishing boats, do not change much over the centuries and I felt a messenger among them, nobody important, just somebody telling some woman spreading out her linen to dry that the farmer's cow had calved or that from the look of the hedges it was going to be a splendid season for blackberries.

The hazard that summer was a practical one. So many of the villagers were away, the men in the navy, the women in the factories, that there was literally a plague of vipers. They coiled themselves about the roots of the trees, they slid along the tops of the banks. One girl was badly bitten on the very edge of the shore. Yet it was a cold, wet summer, the military had barred us from most of the coastal paths but they had left us the lanes; these had become strange and unexpected gardens full of ferns and foxgloves while the formerly gay cottage borders were planted sternly with cabbages or potatoes.

I went for long walks almost every day. It was permissible then to think about the past in a way that was impossible in London. Cornwall had given me the gift I most desired when I was young, friendship with a writer. There is one moment and one moment only when a beginner discovers what is new and contemporary in the art around him and this came for me when I discovered H.D.'s *Sea Garden* in 1917. I learned all the poems by heart, I repeated them to myself throughout that dark and terrible time (as I have written, it was so much worse than the Second War) and we finally met that summer when she was staying near the Land's End. It was only later that we discovered we were cousins, rather tenuous ones but cousins all the same because a Puritan ancestor of hers had gone to America for religious reasons almost two centuries before and later, much later, the descendants got tangled up in some way with cousins of my father. It was the Puritan element, a matter of conscience and principle, that had now kept Hilda in London. "It was here that people first read my poetry," she said, "I am staying with them." So she sat at her typewriter throughout the Blitz, working and writing in spite of the raids. She had such a keen sense of hearing and was so sensitive to the slightest sound that I never understood how she not only managed to endure the noise but to write some of her finest poetry in spite of it. Now as I walked across the fields, I kept on thinking of the day I had knocked on her door and looked up for the first time into her eyes that were sometimes blue, sometimes almost the green of the waves that sweep gently across the sands of the islands she loved so much, and heard her asking me to come into her room in a voice that remains with me as the most beautiful one that I have ever heard. It was not only a door that opened that day but the beginning of so many friendships and adventures, because without her I should never have met Osbert, Edith or Kenneth, Norman, Marianne Moore, Sylvia, Adrienne and so many other friends. She was a messenger and seer like no other person I have known; later I took her to the Scillies, she took me to Greece. Now for the "days of Mars" we were together "inside the citadel" as many people called London, near the park guns and, though we did not know it then, an unexploded bomb. It is the poets who are the leaders of the people. She could have left us easily, but she stayed.

1944

It was a year of problems and disasters.

Norman Pearson returned towards the end of January, after an absence in Spain and Portugal, bearing two bananas, two oranges and a pineapple. The bananas and oranges were simple, Hilda and I had one each. Apart from a few green apples and some berries in Cornwall, it was the first fruit that we had tasted for two years. It seemed so unreal that we hardly liked to touch it. The pineapple was different. Even Hilda, the recluse, agreed that we could not eat it alone and that, wartime or not, it called for a party.

By the time that I had telephoned, written notes or gone round in person with the invitations, we managed to collect about twenty people and how we all got into our little sitting room at Lowndes remains a mystery. First we looked respectfully at the pineapple, then with infinite solemnity it was sliced into tiny mouthfuls. We could now boast for a week afterwards, "Oh, the powder in the rations tastes so much better if you mix it with a little fruit." Norman seemed startled by the result of his generosity but swallowing our separate morsels, they were a symbol that one day the war might end. Our pineapple belonged to the real world of sun and sea with no Government directives and all of us felt the better for our inch of it. It was people who mattered in the war and how much more work the officials would have got out of them if moments of relaxation had been considered as important as their daily tasks. We were willing to face conditions of extreme discomfort but not an endless flow of propaganda that eventually nobody believed. So many difficulties, so much despair, could have been avoided if we had only had psychologists in the upper ranks instead of clerks.

It was the night before Waterloo, because shortly afterwards what came to be called the "Christmas Tree" raids began. These were marked by what appeared to be colored flares. They were harder to endure because of the relatively quiet winter months and a fear as to what might happen the next summer as it was an open secret that preparations for the "Invasion" had begun. However I met in the queue an old lady who had returned from the country who remarked to me, "It was my first raid, dear, last night. I didn't mind the bombs as much as I expected, it was our rocket gun that shook me."

I do not know what we should have done without Norman at this time. He was hardly ever free but when he could, he came in for an hour on Sunday evenings. Then he spoke of poetry to Hilda and of future travel to me. Our resistance was wearing out, we were held by habit to our daily duties but we had almost lost the hope that the war might end. Norman reminded us that there were other things besides ration cards and shortages; in a far-off, hardly to be imagined time there might even be life.

I noted in my diary that I finished the first draft of *Beowulf* on January 18th but it was years before it was published. It came out first in a French translation in Paris through the efforts of Sylvia and Adrienne, then it was issued in America. But England would have none of it, they had had enough of war. The great feat, I felt, was to have written it at all as I had no proper table for the typewriter but only a wide slab underneath a window where I could just balance it. I was dependent on a machine because I had learned to use one when I was fifteen and neither I nor anyone else could read my handwriting.

One February day I saw by chance a new book by Colette in a bookshop window. It had been printed in 1941, the pages were not cut and I wondered how it could have got to England? From Spain perhaps or North Africa? It was, to use an obvious expression, water in the desert. I admired her work, Adrienne Monnier knew her and it was the first modern French book I had seen since I had left Switzerland. At Burier I read as much French as English.

People now often dismiss Colette as old-fashioned. It is the fate of the pioneer. Nobody is more lightly tossed aside by the next generation who enjoy without thinking the victories that their elders won for them at a costly price. Only the survivors who were brought up as I was in the Edwardian tradition can realize what Colette did for us in the way of breaking barriers. It never mattered to me who fell in love with whom in her books, it was an incidental happening, what was important was that she fought for the right of women to live their own lives. She was eighteen years older than I was but little had changed during that time, the clothes, the furniture that she described so vividly had still been part of my Edwardian childhood. She always seemed a contemporary to me, stating my own principles. What we wanted was freedom, no privileges but the same right as men to work at interesting jobs. The First War had opened a few doors but for some reason that I am unable to define (it may be due to the excessive growth of the population) the Second slammed many of them shut again.

I liked Colette's sense of justice, of the air being free (as ours at that raiding moment certainly was not), the way she recalled in a couple of words the feel of a dog's hair, the wash of April rain, the scent of a shrub at dusk. She had her bulldogs, I had my boxers with their squat muzzles and independent scowls and she reminded me of

120

the hours when I had escaped alone into the garden at six o'clock in the morning as a child because that was the only free moment of my day. Our age makes us to some extent and if she fell in love with a boy or a girl or a flower, what did it matter to me? I was in love with freedom. So coming home when it was less the question of whether we could endure till after the invasion than if we could hold out for another week, the book was a fortification (in all the meanings of that word) against the overwhelming grimness of the moment.

Books! They were all we had and whenever I could I went in search of treasure trove to the London Library. I was summoned there one Saturday in March, not to look for material that would ultimately help me to write *The Player's Boy* but because it had been bombed.

There were about a dozen volunteers in the hall when I arrived. They were either very young girls or somewhat ancient gentlemen. Two tired and harassed librarians, both over military age, were in charge of the action. "It's very kind of you to come," one murmured politely to each visitor, "I hope you have brought an apron."

We had. We were all in our oldest overalls with decrepit woolen caps pulled down over our hair. The place was full of the by now familiar smell of stale water, dust and explosives but it was largely the hoses that had done the damage as the Library itself had escaped the hit that had partly demolished the house next door. We were set to work wiping the books and spreading them out one by one on newspapers in the hope that they would dry. People were silent at first, then gradually they began to talk, mostly reminiscences about various raids. I was gloating a little too smugly over the fact that the Elizabethan section had escaped with a mere sprinkling when one of the librarians looked up from a jumble of the wettest books that he was sorting into piles. "I suppose none of you read German?" he asked as if the word itself must be contaminated.

"I do," I said thoughtlessly. German to me meant either the early film days in Berlin before the city was desecrated or else the German-speaking part of Switzerland and I thought sadly that it might be years before I saw my much loved Zurich again.

The librarian looked relieved. He led me over to a pile of books larger and heavier than any I had ever seen, all soaking wet and covered with a thick layer of gray powder. "It's the best of the German encyclopedias," he explained, "but it's in sections and I cannot read the title pages. It's a dreadful mess but I know we can't replace it so if you would do what you can . . ."

Why had I been such a fool? My instinct for adventure was always leading me to jump head foremost into things before considering the possible consequences. Now while the others were gossiping as they worked, I was sneezing violently as I scraped away the dust and getting dirtier and dirtier as I mopped up the water. Nobody shouted gaily across to me as I rolled up my damp sleeves, I was the outcast who knew a forbidden language. I had leisure, however, to decide that I must be far more British than I supposed. I doubted whether a German professor would have given up his one free af-

ternoon to clean some English textbook on botany, for all
the jargon about science being above the ties of nationality. Few of their scientific colleagues had helped my refugees to get away. They had simply grabbed their jobs.
The encyclopedia was also written in such a ponderous
German that a single glance was sufficient to repel the
most enthusiastic of readers. (I have found that if one
wishes to study a difficult subject it is wiser to get a textbook in French, lucidity is the fabric of that language.)
However I read the list of contents and got the set into
reasonable order by the time the librarian came over to
see how I was getting on with the job. Then, refusing the
offer of a cup of tea that would have been taken, I suspected, from his own meager rations, I put on my coat
and walked home to Lowndes.

Whitsun 1944. I read that they were giving a perform-
ance of *A Winter's Tale* in Regent's Park. Theater means
very little to me but I have a perverse fondness for plays
performed in the open air. Then they seem nearer and
less artificial.

I set off on the bus after lunch, reflecting gloomily as
we drove up Baker Street that Authority had succeeded
where the Blitz had failed. It had broken our nerves with
its pre-invasion gloom and despondency. (Why did it
feel that it had to defend its attempt to end the war?) I
sat beside a man who had just bravely bought a poodle in
our era of restrictions and we got into conversation as is
natural with dog lovers. "Do you think tripe is bad for
him?" he asked.

"Tripe? Not if you can get it."

"Or horseflesh?"

"Some vets say it prevents worms and others that it encourages them. In wartime I'm not sure. Don't you find a puppy difficult these days?"

"It just means getting up an hour earlier," and he sighed. Not to get up immediately one woke was one of life's greater luxuries in our usually unheated rooms. I admired him for trying to carry on an ordinary life with the hopefulness and tenacity of a British Bulldog even at the risk of choking on a dehydrated bone.

Regent's Park was full of people, the chestnut blossoms had fallen over the path and all of us (aware that the invasion was near) longed for tall grasses, fields and water. Why, if we could not go to the sea, had they taken the Thames away from us? Our former highway had become the property of grimy barges. Yet the setting was excellent when I got to the theater, trees, a dark thicket and the pale, powdery English sky above our heads. The audience was Elizabethan, small boys drank synthetic lemonade out of jam jars, old ladies folded newspapers into tricornes and stuck them firmly on their gray heads although the sun barely warmed our chairs and there was an ominous notice tacked up on a pole, "Rugs for Hire." Planes roared overhead but lower, at the proper local level, there were birds. Rafe the Apprentice had gone to the wars but the Citizens' Wives were out in force.

All we lacked when the play began was the sense of spoken poetry. You could almost feel the players shudder if they had to keep to the rhythm of a line. The silences between some of Shakespeare's words are as important as the sounds but if people try to use Elizabethan, whether they are actors or teachers, all we get are what Norman Douglas used to call "the vocables" strung together like grunts from some unused tongue. That afternoon the speech was probably not much worse than some I have heard on the great stages of the world but it was simply not Elizabethan. Years later, I actually heard the real language spoken by two scholars. It was exactly as I had heard it in my head. One was Leslie Hotson and the other was a record by the late Helge Kökeritz, *Shakespeare's Pronunciation*. The knowledge is available. It is simply that it lies in an academic corner and most people are unaware of it. How much they miss! If they could only hear it they would understand the plays better and why certain lines scanned in their own period of history but halt in our present tongue.

The sun went in, it got a little colder, there was much fumbling with rugs. I drifted away before the finish but I could not resist leaving a paper at the Box Office, "We are so near the Zoo, couldn't you have borrowed a real bear?"

We appreciate what we have to earn. I loved the occasional weekends at Renishaw or Eckington but the journey was an ordeal. There had not been any recent raids but we felt a loyalty to London and I remember once explaining to the porter that I had to go to Derbyshire on business but should be back the following Monday. "You're lucky to be taking the 12:10. The 2:40 always leaves people behind on Fridays," was his only reply.

I got a good seat that day, not a window one naturally but at least the corner next the corridor (alas, that life should come to mean such petty triumphs!) and watched two young officers stack their belongings and then go out to smoke on the platform. A man put his bowler on the rack and buried himself behind a paper while a woman, obviously from some Ministry, took out a folder of official-looking papers. Then an energetic young woman in W.V.S. uniform (the Women's Volunteer Service, for those who have forgotten wartime terms) appeared, leading an old lady while a porter followed with the baggage. Only the elderly and sick got such attention. "You'll be all right," the girl said briskly as she installed her in the middle seat beside me. "Emma is going to meet you at the station."

"Yes, dear, I shall be all right." It was such a faint whisper that I could hardly hear it although I was such a short distance away.

"I'll put your rug on the rack and I'm sure this lady," W.V.S. looked at me sternly, "will get your thermos down for you whenever you want it."

"I shall wait for tea till I get home," this time the voice was firmer, "but I should like my rug, please."

"Grandmother!" The young woman looked positively horrified, "It's so hot." I could see her as a teacher at some boarding school, flinging up windows and grumbling about stuffiness on an icy, January morning.

126

"For you, dear, but I am happier with something over my knees. There may be a draft when we start."

"I can always put it on the rack for the lady," I suggested, "if she finds she doesn't need it."

"Oh, thanks!" She dumped the folded rug into her grandmother's lap and stood half in the compartment and half in the corridor, looking embarrassed as if she ought to explain to us why she was not at work.

"You have been so kind, dear, seeing me into the train but I know how much you have to do, you mustn't wait."

"They gave me the morning."

"I know, dear, but by the time you've caught your bus and had your lunch it will be two o'clock. Really, I shall be all right and I'll get Emma to telephone this evening."

"If you are sure . . . ," duty was fighting with an obvious desire to get away.

"I shall feel happier if I know I'm not keeping you."

The girl bent down and pecked the old lady's face. "Be sure you tell Emma to phone but I shall be at the canteen till eight. Any time, say, after eight thirty."

"I won't forget, dear."

"Well, goodbye, hope you don't get too tired." She pushed her way briskly between the soldiers standing in the corridor, tapped once on the window and strode away.

Wartime was endurable only as long as we were active and I dreaded the four hours that the journey would take. It was too dark to read inside the station and it rattled too much once the old, overloaded train started. There was a shout, the two officers stamped out their cigarettes and came back to their seats while I had an impulse to say very solemnly, "Do you remember the Brontosaurus? It had a brain the size of a pea and a tail as long as Buckingham Palace but the climate changed suddenly, the marshes dried up and it took so long for a message to get from the tip of its tail to its head that it tumbled into a sandpit and died. That is what is going to happen to us." Alas, who would have listened to me? They would simply have called the guard and told him that all the new talk about secret weapons that was going around seemed to have unhinged my mind.

"You must tell me at once if there is anything that I can do for you," I murmured instead to my neighbor.

"You are very kind but I don't think I shall want anything now that I have my rug." She hesitated and then as if she could not keep the matter to herself any longer, she added, "I was saying goodbye to my grandson before he goes overseas."

I nodded. What kind of encouragement could one give?

"He's going East. He says the war will be over before he gets there but they are not sending him all that way to bring him back at once. At my age, I cannot hope to see him again and he's always been so good to me."

"Oh, you may. They often fly them back these days, it's not necessarily a troopship."

The old lady shook her head. "He was always fond of me but I'm getting on for ninety and I've had my life."

At such moments of truth, sympathy is idiotic and it

must have been to break the tension that the man with the bowler hat remarked quietly, "We are about in the middle of it. I said it would last five years when we left France."

"You were there in 1940?" One of the young officers looked up with interest.

"We brought our rifles back with us although we had to abandon the guns, but we saved the dogs."

"The what?" we yelled in unison.

"The dogs. They joined us whenever we marched through a village, large and small, watchdogs and pets."

"Whereabouts were you?" the other officer asked.

"Where? I wish I knew! We had been detached on liaison duties with the French and we kept moving backwards and forwards with some of their staff. There was a radio blackout and they did not seem to know where they were themselves. We only heard about Dunkirk five days after it happened and then a French general advised us to make for the coast."

"What a mess!"

"It was. Yet all the same I enjoyed that march. We kept tramping from one deserted village to another and it was like living through some extraordinary tale. Even if we found a peasant who had been brave enough to stay in his home, he could only tell us the name of the hamlet. Sometimes he did not know why his neighbors had left or what had happened. But the dogs knew. They fell in and marched beside us as precisely as if they had been drilled."

"And you got away?"

"Yes, it's a strange story and I shall have to wait for the end of the war before I can talk about it."

"Extraordinary affair, the retreat."

"It was! The Germans caught up with us at the end and unfortunately I got a bullet through me so now I'm back with our family business up north. But I managed to bring the regimental funds out with me in my haversack and I suspect some of the animals came as well; it's hard to attend to all the details at such a time. Yet I shall never forget the days we tramped through France nor the scent of the thick grasses in the meadows, the apple trees with the fruit beginning to form, and marching beside us as proudly as if they formed a regiment of their own, the dogs."

How does one feel about an important date in history? I fear nothing at all. On June 6th I went to the bank in Sloane Street to get the weekly supply of petty cash. "It's started," the cashier said and although I had listened to the trucks passing at night for weeks, I wondered for a moment what he meant? We had had so many alarms and inconvenient surprises. "The Invasion," he added, noticing that I looked puzzled. I walked back to tell Hilda but there was no stir in the streets, many had still not heard the news, others could only think about the inevitable losses. Actually most Londoners were too battered by the raids to react at all. The Government, as usual, bungled the announcements. Naturally they could not tell us what was happening along the French coast but this had been a war directed against civilians as much as armies and instead of being determined and confident, they seemed to be apologetic about trying to end it.

About ten days later I had to go to Eckington again and as I had a suitcase full of heavy manuscripts and papers, I was glad to find an elderly porter. There was a feeling of uneasiness everywhere and while we were climbing slowly up a flight of stairs, he put my case down and burst out angrily, "Call this a war, they do. People forget. I've been in three of them and got my four sons in this one. It was the Boer War where the fighting was and I was in the middle of it. Never knew from one moment to the next when some Boer might shoot me."

"It must have been dreadful," I hastily agreed and yet strange as the comment seemed, I wondered if the man was not right? Personal peril overwhelms national dangers and the first time is always the best or the worst. I could remember a detachment of young men marching along the main street of a little seaside town where I had lived when I was four, in the khaki uniforms none of us had previously seen. "Off to Africa, they are," somebody muttered, a woman cried, my nurse told me that many of them might never come home. I was puzzled as to what death was but I was not frightened. So now, looking at the old porter lugging my case to the train when at his age he ought to have been sitting outside some cottage in the sun, the memory of that company seemed far more warlike, although I could not explain why, than lying on the floor at Lowndes with a rug round my head while a bomb set our building rocking as if it had been built out of paper.

Derbyshire looked lovely, it was colder there than in the South and the red May was still in flower in Robert's garden. *Hansard* made the day for me with the report of an elderly member of Parliament who said that he was unwilling "to take the unnecessary risk of persuading Churchill to stay at home." Naturally we began to talk about Sylvia and Adrienne and wonder anxiously if they would survive a Liberation in safety. There would certainly be fighting in the streets. The longer a war lasts the more the extraneous things drop away and it is only friends and perhaps a special corner of a city that count.

Osbert invited me to lunch and for a walk and warned me gently that even if the war ended in a few months, it would still be a long time before I could go home. (He was right, it was almost two years and then I was the second exile on a long list to get back to Vaud.) "Oh, Bryher, the little owls, the little Italian owls, shall we ever hear them again?" I had been thinking selfishly of Burier and forgetting that he longed as much for Montegufoni. Then he continued very seriously, "Your duty now is to get Hilda away. The Germans have got a new missile and you are right in the center, near the park. Take her to the country at once."

That evening the first flying bombs fell on London.

I found Hilda understandably nervous on my return next day. She had faced the first and most terrifying night alone. I suggested that we move at once to Cornwall. We were due to take our annual holiday there in about three weeks. "Leave Lowndes now because of That Man? Never!" She was working on some poems at the time. So we settled down, more gloomily than ever before, to "take it" along with our fellow Londoners. When the folk started calling the bombs "doodlebugs" Hilda, with a poet's love of language, felt better. I could not truthfully say that the name helped me at all. As I wrote to a friend, "One is peacefully typing or eating one's supper, or even sitting of a late afternoon in the park watching old dames exercising their Pekes, there is a noise like an express train and then the earth heaves up and you don't know where you are. Most people say that there is a red light and as it gets over your head, the red light goes out, the tail wags and then you are blown to high heaven but the authorities say no, we exaggerate. Anyhow there are fierce fights between people who would rather have the Blitz and people who would rather face the bugs. I think the bugs are worse myself but it is a moot point. We are pretty evenly divided and as with a real bug, or cockroach, you can't get away from them anywhere."

We forgot the invasion thinking about our own troubles. I had to go to Kingsway one afternoon on some business errand when the alert sounded and without thinking, for the first and only time during the war, I dived into the nearest shelter. I was surprised to find myself sitting there. Was it prescience? The next day a bomb fell in a neighboring street causing some of the heaviest civilian casualties of the war.

We heard that Cole had been taken ill with jaundice and evacuated to some hospital in the country. I begged Hilda again to advance the date of her holiday. She refused. On the 5th of July we heard a "doodlebug" apparently coming in a direct line towards us. We both lay down on the floor. The noise stopped, there seemed to be a moment of complete silence. It was followed by a terrific explosion. Somebody nearby had "had it."

"That must have been near Gerald," I said, "as soon as the all clear goes, I'll ring him up." It was forbidden to telephone during raids. I tried to get him that evening but there was no reply. We were not unduly anxious because the telephone wires might have been cut or he might have already left for his Watch at St. Paul's.

A short time afterwards Andrew Butler telephoned. He was Gerald's great friend, also a member of the Watch and the author of one of the best books about the early raids, *Recording Ruin*. "Bad news," he said at once, "Gerald's flat has been hit, he was there and has lost an eye. The place is wrecked and if Cole had been there she would almost certainly have been killed. Can you meet me outside the Natural History Museum at ten tomorrow? I want you to help me save their things."

Of course we had known people who had lost their homes, an acquaintance had been buried for several hours but Gerald was the first member of our own group to be actually wounded. It was important for friends to dash to the ruins. Wardens had neither the time nor the authority to salvage what was left and unless possessions were rescued quickly, the acids in the dust destroyed them.

We did not have a happy night but I was at the appointed place to meet Mr. Butler the next morning. The Natural History Museum was the center for Civil Defense. Men looked at me suspiciously while I waited outside, I had no right to be there, but Gerald's friend soon tapped me on the shoulder. "Come along, we've got to get this paper signed. I don't know how long that house is going to stand up."

The museum had been one of the haunts of my childhood and the skeletons of great prehistoric beasts still looked down imperturbably at the tiny figures in blue Civil Defense uniforms scattered among lines of school desks among a chaos of telephone wires. The cases full of small dragons had been stored in the basement but the contrast between the arches of bone of the bigger dinosaurs and the people struggling with "incidents" was overpowering. I felt myself turning into a wretched mouse about to be trodden on by some scaly paw that would not be even aware that it had crushed me.

Butler called, we got a taxi to the hospital where they were still dealing with the night's casualties but we were allowed in by special permission. They carried an elderly man past me on a stretcher; whether from shock or injury his face was less white than a curious sulphur yellow and it needed only a glance to see that he was dying. Gerald was lying at the end of a row of beds with a mass of bandages across his face. I felt more frightened than I had ever been in a raid, no doubt because we can stand danger more easily if the mind pretends nothing can happen to us. The heads of the people beyond him, most of them under sedatives, looked like blobs of plaster.

"Sign here," Butler said quietly, guiding Gerald's hand as if he were a child; it was a document that authorized us to enter the flat and save whatever was possible. Then Gerald reached for my hand. He was too ill to be evacuated and the alerts were frequent. "You must go now," the nurse said firmly, "more casualties are coming in." Butler pulled my sleeve. "I'll write Cole," I promised, disengaging myself gently and then a cry came from the doom of the world, "My eye, Bryher, my eye."

Mrs. Ash was helpful but stern. "Wear your oldest clothes, madam, and mind you don't change in your room when you get back. Go straight out to the fire escape, roll up your overall and leave it with your stockings beside the back door. I don't mind washing them all for you but if the grit gets into the lino, I shall never get rid of it."

Why must duty usually be unpleasant? I dreaded the afternoon. There were no suitcases in the stores but after hearing my story, our local tea merchant donated some empty cardboard canisters that were too fragile for the shop to use again. I managed to get a taxi with great difficulty, we picked up the boxes on the way and drove down the Brompton Road. It was completely empty. At first it did not look as if "an incident" had occurred but as we got nearer we saw officials standing in the middle of the street, all the windows in the neighboring buildings had been smashed and there had been many casualties in the house that had been sliced in two on the opposite side of the road. I offered the driver a large tip if he would stay and take the boxes back to Lowndes. Alas, at that moment an alert sounded and he shook his head. "No, madam, I wouldn't stay if you offered me five pounds but you know why this has happened to us, don't you?"

I shook my head.

"It's because we lifted up our hands against our anointed King. We drove King Edward away. It's God's judgment on us."

Nothing erases a deep memory from the folk. It makes national behavior extremely unpredictable and I felt that I had slipped back to the Wars of the Roses.

A girl in slacks came up to us as the cab drove away and I recognized Joan, one of Cole's friends. "Wonderful! Wherever did you find those boxes? We shall need every one of them."

"Now, girls, no chatting." Mr. Butler came over to us from the group in the road. "They're only letting us go inside because I'm an architect and I've promised that we'll be out in an hour."

Mr. Butler had brought a friend and a relative of Gerald with him so we were a party of five. Each of us seized a canister or one of the old suitcases that Joan had managed to collect and we started up the stairs. The steps were difficult to find, they were piled inches high with rubble but the direction was easy. There was the print of a hand in blood all the way down the wall. "Gerald's hand," somebody muttered.

I was the last of the group to enter the sitting room where I had spent so many happy Sunday mornings. It was over a foot deep in plaster, in some cases this came up to our knees and, winding like a river, a deep stain of blood ran through it from the window to the door. Cole's sofa, where she usually sat, had vanished. There was not even a fragment of wood left. Yet the cabinet against the wall a couple of feet away was intact, her china gleaming unharmed behind the polished glass. The rest of the furniture was part of the rubble on the floor, except for half a book dangling from a shelf and one chair that had somehow survived at the back of the room. They knew there was a hole somewhere and Mr. Butler prodded the mess carefully with a stick. "Hurry up, girls," there was a muffled sound somewhere in the distance, it was possibly demolition work but could have been a bomb, "if the noise gets worse, we shall have to run."

Joan and I went into Cole's bedroom and began to stuff clothes, there was no time to fold them, into a suitcase. One of the men did the same with Gerald's things. It was important to save every scrap we could because neither clothes nor linen could be replaced. The worst moment came when we went into the kitchen and saw Cole's little stock of jam, she had made it from sugar saved patiently from her ration month by month, but now it was too broken or full of grit to rescue. Nobody spoke, we all wanted to leave these grim surroundings as soon as possible. Then a surprising thing happened.

It is hard to think of anything more despicable than looting from bombed-out and helpless people yet I found a tiny saucepan such as we had needed for days and that money could not buy, while Joan picked up a skirt. "I gave her that and I don't believe she has ever worn it." When would Cole need to cook again? The apartment could not be repaired for months. In Joan's case the skirt had originally been hers and I was saved from temptation by a shout from Mr. Butler. "Are you ready? Time's up. The sooner we are out of here the better." We shoved the skirt and saucepan into a carton; I have tried not to condemn wrongdoers too hurriedly since. Civilization is never as strong as we pretend.

There was little to be saved from the sitting room except the china. The rest was dust. Somebody yelled from the street below and we started to lug the cases towards the stairs when Joan trod on something soft. She bent down and picked up a lump that looked like a plaster doll. It was only after she had shaken it violently that it turned out to be Cole's favorite fur cap that she had worn for several winters. "I can get it cleaned for her," Joan said, tucking it under her arm but again it brought back the cheerful days when Cole had burst into the flat wearing it on her head. One of the helpers, the relative, had a permit for his car so we were able to load the cases on to it and then, thankful to be out in the sunlight once more, I walked back to Lowndes.

I duly remembered Mrs. Ash's orders and went straight out to the step above the fire escape. Hilda brought me a basin and a pail of water. I scrubbed, later

I had an extra bath (permitted under the circumstances
although we were normally rationed to one a week), but
it was days before I got the grit out of my legs; the grains
of rubble clung like burrs.

Gerald recovered slowly but his knowledge of London
died with the streets that vanished because he could
never write his history or work much again on the archives. If he had been on duty with St. Paul's Watch, he
would probably have been entitled to compensation.
Having been injured in his own home, he got barely
enough to pay the medical expenses. One moment was
granted him after the war. His knowledge of historical
ceremonies proved invaluable at the Coronation in Westminster Abbey in 1953. Otherwise he never really got
over the bombing and died, comparatively young and
during the same year as his wife, in 1962.

If I am in England, I walk sometimes in his memory
on a Sunday morning through the quiet City streets (he
would never recognize them now) regretting with deep
sadness that he was unable to write the story of them he
had planned.

Hilda and I left for Cornwall as arranged on the 20th
of July. We got to the station early and lined up among
the front ranks of a waiting crowd under the glass roof
when an alert went. "Passengers are advised to go to shelters," a voice bellowed through the loud-speaker but
were we going to lose our places so painfully acquired in
the queue? No! Soldiers could indulge in strategic with-

drawals according to plan, but British Bulldog families on their annual holiday were holding their ground to the last baby and the last pram.

The train drew in. It was a moment when Hilda's long legs were invaluable. She ran forward as if competing in a Greek foot race and won us two corner seats. I lumbered after her with the baggage. The other four people in the compartment were a Guard's officer who had lost part of a hand, a lady who was apparently his aunt and had just left the hospital after an operation, and a young R.A.F. clergyman and his wildly inappropriate fiancée who looked as if she had stepped straight from the cover of one of the more lurid peacetime movie magazines. She dangled in his arms, yes, literally in his arms as if she were rehearsing a scene for a film while he alternately stroked her when he could free his hand or did conjuring tricks with match-boxes and half crowns for our amusement. He was taking her to Plymouth to introduce her to his mother and as the officer remarked once they had left the carriage, "She had the wind up good and proper."

Directly they left us the aunt took over. "When Jerry, I mean the Germans, took me for a spy in the last war, you see, I was nursing in Belgium and they told us not to take photographs but you know . . . ," girlish giggle, "when I am forbidden to do things, oh, I know it's very wicked of me but I just have to disobey so I did take photographs. . . ." I never heard what subsequently happened because at that moment the ticket collector came round and after he left she whispered to me that people ought to be very reserved in public places and followed up the remark by telling me the story of her life in detail. "I never dare permit myself to become attached to anyone for then I always lose them, there was my darling little dog . . . ," she took out her handkerchief and I moaned in sympathy, after four years my boxer would have forgotten me if I did get back to Switzerland, and then we discussed whether there was a dog's heaven and if they had souls? I dared not whisper that it must be bad enough to be a dog without having the inconvenience of a soul on top of it.

Two évacuée mothers and their two small boys replaced the clergyman and his fiancée at Plymouth. The boys played "machine guns" up and down the crowded corridor, pointing at each other and shouting "You're dead." It prompted the officer to remark that recently he had been instructor of a Canadian detachment at a battle school near London but it had had to be moved because the tiny tots of the neighborhood had been quicker than his soldiers. They had popped up from all the right strategic places to pelt his men with rotten tomatoes, bottle glass and homemade grenades. One immense Guardsman was within grabbing reach when they all disappeared except for one five-year-old who stuck his tongue out, stood his ground and disappeared into a carefully prepared hole just as a stick descended. Finally they had had to move the school. It was surely one of the best stories of the war.

There was a shout of "Tea" at the next station so the soldier and I jumped out and charged down the platform towards the urn. It was a feat needing the utmost delicacy and judgment to carry two over-full cups and purse through the crowds, and some tea got spilled in the process. The soldier handed his spare cup to his aunt, I gave one of mine to Hilda. Alas, then I had to do a Sir Philip Sidney and offer my own to an évacuée mother who looked as if she were about to faint. It seemed easier than trying to revive her. The soldier then insisted that I take his cup, saying it would give him an excuse to unscrew his whisky flask but he was not the drinking type and I think it was pure kindness.

His aunt remarked that all she asked for now in life was "a cup of tea, an egg (for she really did not care for meat), a cigarette and a good book." Naturally I asked her at once what books she preferred? Well, her favorite was Stanley Weyman, she had read *A Gentleman of France* five times, she liked Hutchinson's *If Winter Comes*, a good natural book about a good natural family because she really couldn't read love stories. *Gone With the Wind* was too long and she must confess too highbrow. Did I read? Well, no, I explained, there wasn't much time for it in wartime, was there? I liked a good biography now and then if it were written in a light, gay manner, I was not much good at heavy reading. "Ah," said Auntie, "I've often wished I could write, it must be wonderful to put sentences together, to say one's thoughts, and one would never be lonely living with one's characters." I agreed, it must be marvelous but didn't she think writing was one of the great mysteries? I could not imagine how people were able to do it.

They got out at the next station and as they walked

down the platform, Hilda leaned forward and said icily, "Bryher, you ought to be smacked."

A delightful old Cornish couple arrived in their place. They had been "directed" to do two years' war work in a remote part of the Orkneys where they had suffered terribly from the cold after the warm West Country air. They looked too elderly to have been called up at all, they had had to change steamers and trains twelve times to get home but once back in their own village they hoped never to leave again while they lived. It was obvious that they had been the prey of one of those muddles that sound so gay in a Compton Mackenzie story but are a tragedy in real life. To be without influence and lost in the wrong filing system meant that the word "justice" might as well be forgotten and hope transferred till the end of the war.

Finally it was our turn to get out after one of the most hilarious journeys I ever remember. Doris was waiting for us and drove us back through the summer scented fields and the occasional glimpses of a blue, Cornish sea, to her farm.

How little we remember of what seems important afterwards. By the time we returned from Cornwall the raids had ceased and the exodus from London began. People who had been loyal to the city as long as there was danger now wanted to get away from the smells and the dust. Early that autumn we said goodbye to Selina and her partner. The building had been repaired but the Government had taken over the *Warming Pan* for a canteen. They had got a reasonable sum, they said, as compensation. It was impossible to open a new restaurant in wartime so they were going to the country to look after an aged relative. I cannot recall much about this last visit except that like everyone else we wondered how much more we had to endure before the peace? I saw Selina once or twice again on rare visits to London but we corresponded regularly until she was killed in a car accident some years later.

The next to leave was George Plank. He was not young and he had never recovered from the severe hardships of his years with the Home Guard when he had spent nights in the open, digging ditches. We suspected that he had never given his real age when he had joined it. Now he had got permission to go to his sister in Pennsylvania for six months. The submarine menace was almost at an end but precautions were still enforced and as with so many he simply disappeared but this time with a happy ending. He recovered much of his health in America and returned the following year to live in his little house in Sussex till he died.

Edith and Osbert came to London for a long visit, Norman did his best to cheer us but we were too exhausted to react except with a dull weariness; apart from the very young, few of us *wanted* to live. The only moment that autumn that broke through our apathy was when we crowded the cinemas to see the film of the Liberation of Paris. The streets stirred memories, they were familiar but were they real? There were crowds, a woman sprawled on the pavement with a bullet through her, passers-by huddled in doorways or were lying in the gutter, it was like turning the pages of an old, discarded magazine. For the first time, I wondered what my own return would be like but this feeling was immediately obliterated by rage. "I told you so in 1932," I wanted to yell. Nobody now could give me back the years I had lost. It was only routine that was holding us together and once it broke (it was easing already as the bombing halted), everything snapped. People quarreled mercilessly with those for whom they had made great sacrifices and the worst in us all came to the surface.

On December 13th, it was a gift that redeemed the bitterness of the closing season, I got my first letter for five years from Sylvia Beach.

1945

This was a cold year of some hope and much disillusionment.

There were icy winds and snow throughout the winter but spring brought a spirit of change. Deliverance was near but not knowing the exact date it would come made us bad-tempered and angry without cause. Families were afraid of their relatives' being killed in the last battles, others feared a final air raid on London. Some supposed that we should revert to the plenty of 1939 immediately the fighting ceased. I knew that this was impossible. The gaiety of the formerly patient queues was replaced by an ugly discontent.

Perdita went off to Paris in March, resplendent in American uniform, promising to send news of Sylvia Beach if possible. We estimated that it would have taken all her clothes coupons for four years to get such equipment in civilian life. Gay letters soon began to reach us. Her work was hard but it was a "liberation" after London. I began to think again of Burier myself.

It was only at weekends that I could escape from my various tasks. Occasionally instead of going to Aldermanbury, I walked directly to the Chelsea side of the river. Wherever it was, the Thames led to the sea. Vision is young, its values are moments and often lines of Mallarmé came into my head as I was wandering beside *"la belle Tamise"* on those Sunday afternoons. I do not know why Mallarmé had captured me so completely when I was eighteen except that he was the poet of the Absolute. Later it was his search, less for the right word than for a deeper emotion. He was a sailor (alas, I heard a few weeks later that the Germans had sunk his famous yacht) and I knew that he had navigated an original way through the imaginative mind. So I murmured lines of his poetry to myself while the Thames flowed beside me, remembering that, peace or war, each of us has a particular conflict to endure. Think of the years that Mallarmé spent teaching English to turbulent French schoolboys instead of being able to concentrate upon his own work! His vision had been part of my "Survival Kit" since I was young and at this time of crisis still kept "Doom and

Despondency," as the posters put it, at bay. Thanks to him, I saw myself as a cabin-boy trotting along the ruins of London, fists clenched, battle-ready, a unit among a million but bitterly aware that nothing now could give me back the years that the Appeasers had wrecked.

There were other experiences besides poetry along the river. I walked further than usual one Sunday beside a waste of dust. There were no wild flowers nor even many broken stones but suddenly an empty building appeared, narrow and high, somehow a more vivid symbol of destruction than a complete ruin. It was just a mid-Victorian house leaning drunkenly towards a by-now nonexistent neighbor. At almost the same moment I was aware of a room cluttered with dark, massive furniture and two elderly ladies sitting beside a fireplace, listening for a bell. There was a feeling of deep apprehension in the room. They were waiting for a nephew who had just returned from India. Financially they were in his power. What would he be like? Would he force them to leave their home? They had not seen him for many years.

It was the anxiety that I felt, rather than a visual image and it was far off in time. I wondered, without being anxious about it, if I had lost my wits? (You can't lose what you haven't got, unsympathetic friends would say.) Then I looked at the river and back to the street and only the house was there, dusty and broken. Eventually I remembered a story that I had read as a small child. It had not been a particular favorite and I had not thought of it for over thirty years but it had been about two old ladies waiting in just such a house. I suppose I must have wondered why they were anxious? According to my experience then, grown-ups could do what they liked. Perhaps there had even been an illustration of a similar building.

So, I thought, this was what the war was making of us, it was giving us hallucinations and driving us back to the blank spaces of our beginnings. My imagination was doubling round and round on itself, like a bird off course.

During the raids it had been a matter of principle to stay and "stick it." Now we all felt that we had to get away. In April, Robert, Hilda and I decided to go to Stratford-on-Avon to celebrate Shakespeare's birthday. I think it was Robert who had the initial idea and presumably because it was wartime we managed not only to get rooms at a hotel but seats at the theater. It was an experience that none of us can have again because that year it was truly a festival of the people, there was nothing either conventional or ambassadorial about it. We came from cities, camps and the adjoining villages for love of Shakespeare and with him, on this particular occasion, England.

I had passed through Stratford for a day when I was about ten but remembered little about it. In 1945 it was not only the ceremonies but also the countryside. The banks of the streams were thick with primroses, the cottagers were beginning to get their gardens back into shape and where the beds were full of lettuces, they were masked in April by the flowering shrubs. We murmured to each other across the hedges and the banks of tiny, wild violets, "No more bombs." It felt already as if peace had come.

Robert and I went for long walks, Hilda meditated in the public gardens, there was more food in the hotel than we had seen for a long time because they had obtained an extra allowance for the festival. During these few days we did not have to queue up with our baskets and carry the rations home, all ordinary existence dropped away and we felt, very proudly, like Elizabethans ourselves.

If it were the wish of any artist to paint the spirit of a country emerging from almost six years of war, he had a blueprint in the procession to the church on Shakespeare's birthday. Almost everybody was carrying a tribute, mostly from their own gardens. Robert was beside me, holding a small bunch to be laid on the stone, Hilda was just beyond him and on my other side was a young soldier in khaki grasping a handful of wildflowers that he had evidently just gathered. We walked slowly along the main street and I was thinking, I am sure, the same thoughts as my neighbors. We had stuck it somehow as England had stuck it at the time of the Armada. The flowers were masking the smell of the polluted London dust and we felt in a way that we could not explain that Shakespeare had helped to pull us through so that we were alive this April morning and we were taking him primroses in remembrance, the flowers that are the first a lot of children recognize by name, from his Warwickshire lanes. We marched in silence, in as near a unity of joy as I have ever experienced in a crowd; there were hundreds of us and the only whisper was the "Thank you" from the man who took our flowers, until we left the church gate. It was a religious experience, one of the most profound I have ever known and the only recognition most of us would have. The Appeasers had let us down, the authorities had tempered the news to suit their own ends but the poets had stayed with us. It was they who, as messengers from the gods, had held.

The Elizabethan world still remained about me. I had another strange experience when I went to see the Shakespeare play in Regent's Park; this year it was *As You Like It*.

I suppose by now I had really learned a great deal about the period and often muttered Elizabethan to myself from which I feel much of modern American is derived. If so, it is likely that the words were taken across the Atlantic by sailors rather than settlers. It was natural enough, I was living more in that century than in wartime London and as well banging about with a folder of papers or a shopping basket and answering quips in the crowd. If people want to learn what sixteenth-century London was like, perhaps the best guide is *The Elizabethan Underworld* edited by A. V. Judges.

The play had one advantage that summer. The actors could not speak blank verse, it is really very difficult, but due to the "call-up" the Duke was an elderly man and Orlando was actually a boy. I had seen a couple of Shakespeare's plays during the winter in the West End theaters, beautifully done, but although I had watched them with interest it was as a twentieth-century spectator and I had remained cool and unmoved. Now, suddenly the wit of the comedy gripped me. I laughed as I have never laughed in any theater before or since. "It's so funny," I tried to explain to my astonished neighbor who had not, apparently, understood a single one of the jokes. All that had happened was that I had read Elizabethan intensely and continuously and was also seeing the play among what could have been an original audience of apple sellers and citizens. Do not mistake me, I had not slipped back in time although for a moment I almost felt I had; it was because the conditions that afternoon cannot have been very different from Shakespeare's time; we faced the ending of an age, the slowing down of a great period of expansion and exploration and this brought with it a fear of the future. I was so soaked in the atmosphere at that moment that I understood the words instinctively, through the heart, not the mind. A couple of years later I read *As You Like It* again; by then I had forgotten what the jokes meant and they seemed pointless and obscure. A play is more dependent than any other imaginative work on the moment when it is produced and can only appeal with the same freshness to its public if the outward circumstances are roughly the same.

I can only record what happened as faithfully as possible. My knowledge of Elizabethan came to me during two wars and seemed to vanish "into thin air" when they were over. Somebody asked me recently the date of Shakespeare's birth and I could not remember it. Now it is as if a sponge had washed the meanings of lines I once knew by heart completely from my mind. Yet I suspect that if the same conditions should recur, Elizabethan with its richness and reassurance would come back to me. In everyday life with quite other frustrations, once I had finished *The Player's Boy,* the age seemed to vanish.

The English made many mistakes during the war but the greatest was in the way they announced peace. They preached to the populace instead of giving it an outlet for its feeling. We had been pent up for almost six years, tons of explosives had been dropped on us without our having a chance to heave even a snowball back and now we were to observe decorum and all but requested to feel sorrow for the enemy! Most of the muddles and difficulties of the following years can be traced back to this incredible blunder.

Saturday, May 5th. We knew that peace was at hand but until the official announcement how could we believe it had come? We were wary because we had been trapped too often by dubious reports. Our first reaction was what should we do about food because the stores would close at once? By ten o'clock that morning they were already sold out of bread. Together with most of the other women in the neighborhood, we went round distributing "Victory tips" to the girls in the shops. Many of them had spent four and five hours a day waiting for the occasional bus to take them to and from work and they had earned their reward.

Nothing happened. "Another rumor!" We shrugged our shoulders and tried to treat it as an ordinary day. In the afternoon Robert, Hilda and I went through pouring rain to see *The Duchess of Malfi;* at such a moment it seemed apt. There was no lightheartedness anywhere in the streets as we went home, the crowds at the bus stops appeared unhappy and puzzled.

Sunday, May 6th. I spent the morning on a round of "Happy Peace" visits. There were only two topics of conversation, "When will the news break?" or "If they close the shops as they say for three days, will they let us get our rations in advance?" I had tea with Philip and discussed the future, it would have been hard to decide which of us was the more gloomy. "This is simply a pause," he said. "The next years are going to be unsettled and very difficult."

Norman came to dinner, we spoke of our pineapple party and then I left him to cheer up Hilda while I dismantled our invasion chest as a symbol and put away the contents. We had had orders always to keep a week's supply in tins in case of an invasion. These were to be changed every few months but otherwise never touched. We agreed that Perdita, she was with the American army somewhere near Germany, was going to see most of the fun. Then we listened solemnly to the nine o'clock news but the announcer sounded as baffled as we were. It was rapidly becoming a nightmare.

Monday, May 7th. I dashed out to queue up before the shops opened but there were already numbers of people in front of me. Neighbors were grumbling that their bread had gone stale on them because as the news had not broken, they could not give their expected party. Most of us planned to share the celebration with friends. I got a loaf and actually a few scones but once back at Lowndes the telephone kept ringing, "Thought you'd like to know, they're breaking the news at four." Immediately after lunch I got on a bus, for a wonder it was half empty, and went as far as St. Paul's. I got off there, walked in pilgrimage along Silver Street, past the site of Shakespeare's supposed lodgings, on to Aldermanbury and the ruins of the church, round to bow to Shakespeare's bust in the little garden and back along Roman London and the Wall to the cathedral where I persuaded an immensely suspicious verger to fetch Gerald. I sat, looking at craters and charred stones for a long time before he arrived.

It was hard to look at Gerald with the black patch over his lost eye and to think of the research that he could now never do. Cole was with friends and we wanted him to join us for the announcement. It was already a quarter past three. The buses were jammed but by sheer luck we found a taxi and when we got to Lowndes, Osbert was also there. Edith was at Renishaw and so he had chosen to be with us. It was a token of affection of which I was very proud. We were all solemn at first but it turned afterwards into one of the most hilarious parties of my life even if it were not the way I had imagined hearing of victory.

We had trouble at first with the radio. We dared not turn it off because of a superstitious feeling that we wanted to hear the official declaration. The B.B.C. rose to the occasion by not varying its program by one minute.

First we had the Children's Hour. I looked round at the faces, really in bewilderment. After all we had endured it was too much. We might now be a German province with most of us dead and here we waited, a poet, a master of English prose, a historian of old London and my messenger-boy self, straining with the rest of the adult population to hear one simple sentence, "The war is over." We were compelled instead to listen at a turning point of our history, to tinkling nursery rhymes and a good night to the little ones. Of course programs cannot be changed in the ordinary course of events but if the Government withheld the news the B.B.C. could have explained this quietly to the waiting multitudes. It was a presage of the muddles that awaited us in the years ahead. The minutes went by, Osbert and Gerald grew wittier and wittier with regard to the situation. Hilda was impatient while I remembered the truly savage outbreak of joy in 1918. At that time Doris and I had had to link arms with complete strangers to avoid being knocked down in the crowd, a few yards away from home.

The children were advised to go happily to bed. We waited. Nothing happened. Hilda managed to find something for the others to drink. We turned the radio as low as we dared and then instinctively one of us would turn it up again. It was long past four. There was a pause. "It's coming!" We clustered round the wireless while something like a movie of the last miserable years flashed across my mind: standing in front of a table at the Food Office; the rattling gunfire that meant that enemy planes were nearing the park. "It's coming!" In an otherwise complete silence the news began in Welsh. Unhappily it was a language none of us understood.

Light music followed. It hardly matched our mood. We ran over our sources of information from very high (Osbert), through church circles (Gerald), to picked-up-in-the-crowds (self). Our visitors discussed the history of Ludgate Hill from prehistoric times to the last raid. We went over every possible hitch, was it a ruse, perhaps the enemy were at the Channel ports again, Pegasus carried us to the utmost limits of fancy.

The announcer announced he had no announcement to make.

Most Londoners were in a state of sullen anger by that time. Osbert left to keep an appointment. Gerald stayed to help Hilda put up our flags. The other apartments were already decorated. Hilda had a huge Stars and Stripes that completely covered the window in her room, I had procured a Welsh Dragon and a Union Jack. Then Gerald left but I turned on the radio again till supper; surely something must happen?

I was so restless that I went out after we had finished our meal and wandered round Knightsbridge. People were shouting mockingly, "It's all over till tomorrow" as they got their buses home. In a fury, because they had no right to work up the feelings of the populace and then not give it even a chip of dog biscuit, I went back to Lowndes. The church bells started and that made the cook next door tap and ask me if I had heard anything. I said "No" but just at that minute our telephone rang and a friend called us to say, "It's peace. They broke into the program to tell us at a quarter to eight." "Always too little, too late" as we used to mutter in the queues. Few things in the war can have been so badly bungled.

Tuesday, May 8th. The first thing that the radio announced was that the bakers would be open for an hour so I dashed out to secure another loaf. It was as calm and silent everywhere as on a Sunday morning. We started telephoning to each other, "How wonderful of you to manage to survive" (as if we had had any choice in the matter!) and Robert asked Hilda and myself to go to his house in Chelsea at three o'clock to hear Churchill broadcast. I left Hilda to go there by herself. I wanted something more adventurous and after waiting half an hour got a Number 9 bus, wedged in with a lot of Wrens with cockades in their hats, and went as far as Aldwych. There I transferred to a Number 11, the last that the police were letting through on the normal route. I raced to the top and in common with everyone else stood on the seats as we went slowly past Trafalgar Square. It was exactly forty minutes past two. The crowds were dense, there were children over all the Landseer lions, not even a paw of one was visible. A lot of French were drawn up in a block at the top of the square. We turned along Whitehall, one army detachment after another was drawn up in the empty spaces and one A.T.S. girl fainted and was dragged to an ambulance to the derision of the crowd. There were flags everywhere but the people were far too sedate. I said as much to my neighbor and he nodded. "Last time I was at sea but this looks to me pretty quiet." The conductor struggled up the steps and implored us to get down from the seats. Joyfully, we took no notice. He could not report us today and we knew it. There were people clinging to every statue. I managed to get off in the King's Road and by wriggling and running got to Robert's house just in time for the broadcast. Hilda had already arrived. He had put out window boxes defiantly filled with petunias and geraniums, and banners were hanging from every window. As a final touch, he had hung a white one over the front door to signify that he could not bear the suspense of waiting for the announcement any longer. "However did you get all the flags?" I asked. They had disappeared weeks before from the shops.

"Oh, every time we had a major disaster I bought a flag to be ready for V Day" was Robert's cheerful reply.

We listened to the broadcast but my thoughts wandered. If the war was over, I could go home. I thought of the woods round Renishaw and wondered what Doris was doing in Cornwall and how strange it would seem not to stand in queues. Robert gave us a wonderful Victory tea and then we walked back; the buses were so crowded that they were not even attempting to stop. The tiny Chelsea streets that had suffered so badly in the raids were a mass of flags but there was still a strange quietness in the air. Everybody had put on not what was suitable but their brightest clothes, red for preference with bright blue as their second choice. I had on my best blue coat and skirt, now seven years old and a red and cream gingham shirt chosen for warmth rather than appearance. I also had the regulation red, white and blue handkerchief in my pocket. Yet the ferocious gaiety of 1918 was missing. That November, people had climbed up into strange balconies and taken over all transport. Still, planes did Victory rolls overhead, people called them sparrows or gulls, cyclists had painted their machines and later when I went into the park, people were lighting spirit lamps and cooking meals. I returned to find Norman making a solemn call on Hilda and he drew my attention to a major difference between England and the States. It surprised him to find the Union Jack painted on biscuit tins, cut up into clothes for the younger children because flags were not on coupons, and he had even found fire watchers using them as extra blankets on a cold night. I explained that what we could not do was to put a crown on anything. I should have liked to fly the Cornish flag but the only one available was the royal one with a crown on it and therefore strictly forbidden. To end the evening we celebrated by opening a tin of hoarded fruit juice, pulling back all the curtains and turning on the lights. It was the first time for almost six years.

Wednesday, May 9th. The first job in the morning was to ring up friends and hear about their adventures. Gerald reported hundreds of people at St. Paul's but added that they had been mostly sightseers who had messed up the steps by sitting there to eat sandwiches. He had had a very long day and had then been unable to get a drink between there and his home which had greatly annoyed him. Supplies everywhere were short, some said because the authorities wanted to keep us quiet. Still he had seen, he said, one of the most amusing sights of the war. A crowd of women had climbed up the Eros statue in Piccadilly but had been sternly ordered down by the police. It was easy to get up but hard to get down, especially as a crowd of soldiers had rushed up with cameras to snap the scene; they had ripped their clothes and had had finally to drop into the arms of the waiting police. If one will climb statues, it is what happens.

Robert had ended up at Whitehall where Churchill on a balcony had conducted the singing of popular songs with his cigar. Churchill had shouted to the crowd, "It's your war" and got the biggest cheers of the day. Then, Robert reported, he himself finished up the evening dancing with a policewoman before going back to Chelsea.

There was nothing that resembled the spontaneous joy of the Armistice of 1918. We had had too many "directives" and too much powdered food. It would have been better for the future if the Government had driven the people into more excesses so as to release the pent-up anger that was to harass the English scene for the following years.

Hilda went off to spend a brief holiday alone at Stratford-on-Avon although as the regulations forbade hotels to keep guests more than four days, she had to move from place to place. I do not know if she actually wrote there some of the poem, "Good Frend," that was afterward published in *By Avon River* but it was certainly in her thoughts. Claribel, King Alonso's daughter in *The Tem-*

pest, married to the King of Tunis and left in a foreign land might have been some reflection of her own experience translated into Elizabethan terms. Had Hilda not been born in Pennsylvania, married to an Englishman in 1913 but treated throughout the First War almost as if she were an alien, and now in the second one "come home" through sharing it and offering her tribute, on that just-past April day, to Shakespeare? I knew that she wanted to be alone on this visit, I could hear her saying to herself, "It's over" as she wandered along the Warwickshire lanes during this first moment of what we called the "almost Peace" because we still expected a long conflict in the East. We had had our "Tempest" and it had passed. People were taking down the blackout curtains and hanging up their pictures. It is sad that so many of her admirers never saw her as I saw her at the peak of her beauty. When I met her first she made me think of the seas around my much-loved Scillies, her eyes would be a clear blue that when the light caught them turned to the green that is only visible when waves wash over sands. She had the limbs of a Greek runner and I never heard anyone read poetry as she read it. The war almost killed her body but never her spirit.

We do seek inspiration in the past; this is a fact, not a theory. The crowds around me were interested in the Elizabethan age, a moment, we all recognized, nearest to our own battle. Yet it is not a period they really understand; to them it was a moment of license and freedom whereas actually it was an epoch that was often austere and always strict. There are sneers in Aphra Behn's plays a couple of generations later about the stern morality of Elizabethan grandmothers. It was the rigidity of life at home that drove the wilder spirits of the time to fight beside the Huguenots in France or against the Spaniards in the Indies. It was also a harsher period than people imagine, there was much disease, many outbreaks of plague and though many children were born, few lived to maturity. Yet poetry is born of danger and whether it was the risk of the Armada or our own raids, people clung to art as they never would have clung to it in peace. Was it a feeling, I wondered, that it might be a form of immortality, an assurance of continuity that might otherwise be lost?

I myself was absorbed by both Ralegh's poetry and life. Now that our own peace conflicts were beginning to emerge, he seemed the modern figure among the Elizabethans. King James and his intrigues with the Spaniards reminded me so much of our Appeasers of the Thirties that I sometimes slammed my books down on the table and wondered if History must always repeat itself?

The populace, heroic as it had been both at the time of the Armada and our own great raids, had to take a part of the blame. It is an extraordinary fact but the English have always behaved the worst to those who have served them best. Drake and Nelson escaped because they conveniently died, it was therefore proper to rank them as heroes. Grenville was suspect but as he perished eventually on a Spanish galleon and the *Revenge* was sunk, he could be tolerated with a shake of the head. Ralegh, the poet, the statesman, explorer and scientist, the man who might have made a second United States out of part of South America, is read and understood today chiefly by scholars. It is true that now our national character has become somewhat milder. Ralegh was beheaded on Tower Hill, Churchill merely got a kick in the pants. Yet history is still the best guide to life if it is only studied carefully. Never expect morality or justice to succeed; it is the parasites who win riches and a comfortable old age, seldom the worthy citizens. Scheme, wriggle and bargain but beware of telling the truth and above all, never be a hero. It is an unwise affectation, particularly after a war.

This year it was possible to go early to Cornwall. I went to stay with Doris on her farm on June 28th and remained until August 16th. It was the longest time that I had been away from London since my arrival from Switzerland in September 1940. Hilda came for a few weeks later and stayed at Tregoning, a smaller house nearer to the village. I wandered about the fields and down to the shore but now I could think of nothing but the Norman Conquest and how it had almost repeated itself in 1940. I had been familiar with the main events since I had read Henty's *Wulf the Saxon* when I was nine, and at fifteen I had devoured Freeman's five-volume history. I suspect that as I was sent to boarding school shortly afterwards, and Queenwood still seems to me one of the shattering events of life, some tinge of the relationship between conquered Saxon and arrogant Norman entered at the time into my own so suddenly changed existence. I seldom thought about the period afterwards until I arrived in London in 1940. Then, and I mean this seriously, after all I had seen some of the effects of defeat coming through France, I combed the libraries for all the books I could find on the subject as a guide in case of possible invasion. It was a help to me personally but I was surprised by the length of time it takes recent discoveries to penetrate the schools. Such are the long reaching effects of propaganda that the average Englishman even today believes that the Normans brought a higher culture into England. He may be remembering pleasant holidays in Normandy but that is a very different land now to what it was a thousand years ago. At the time of the Conquest the Normans were the Nazis of their time, there had been such long and continuous fighting in their own country that they had wasted their own and the surrounding provinces until starvation was common. They were hungry, they had everything to gain and nothing to lose by seizing London. The English on the contrary were rich, there were several centers of art and learning, much of it subsequently lost, and apart from the Welsh Marches and the North Coast they were sleepy with peace. Few of the leaders of that time, apart from Harold, were men of action. It took England more than a century to regain even a part of the culture that was destroyed. The Normans knew that they had to win or starve and remembering Munich and our own near-defeat, I found a study of the period gloomy but instructive.

So I roamed the still-empty fields and the story of *The Fourteenth of October* did not come into my head as

166

much as it unrolled itself, with the regular movement of the waves across the sand, exactly as if it were happening in front of me. Sometimes I wondered if an emotion could brand itself upon a place, I felt the desolation of that conquered time so strongly. Our war had been almost a repetition of 1066 except that now, in 1945, we had a form of "happy ending." Was this because England was now an entity instead of the several provinces more or less isolated from each other that it had been in the eleventh century? Perhaps if we are free today instead of being a Nazi dependency, our survival is due to the ease of modern communications and to our relationship with other countries, particularly America. Warnings were not restricted as in 1066 to the speed of runners or the occasional rider.

The countryside that summer seemed to have a beauty I have never known before or since. The tall pink campion thrust upwards on the banks between the wild, white roses. Grass was springing along the unused wheel ruts and it was the year the foxgloves came. The summer before, few were in flower; the next year they would be gone but for this one moment they swept up the cliffs in waves, red with white foam flecks at the center of each flower. Little hawks were rising in the air above them but the shore was empty. Nature had taken back the beaches for itself.

There was peace in Europe. It brought new problems although now we could walk to Godrevy beach and bathe with a clear conscience. Letters came more frequently from Sylvia and Adrienne, they were both ill, Sylvia had been interned for a time and they were still short of food and medicine. Their apartments were safe but the lease of the bookshop had lapsed and there would be no chance to reopen it. I heard from Elsie in Vaud, the dogs had survived and I had begun the formalities to get a permit to return to Burier. My lawyer warned me it might take a year, actually it took eight months. Meanwhile I was free to wander a little but wherever I walked, the plight of the English after Hastings came constantly into my mind. A few of the lucky ones fled to France, a separate kingdom at that time, and tried there to hire themselves out as mercenaries. Many had joined the Varangian Guard. There is said to be information about them in the Byzantine archives at Istanbul. It seems not to interest scholars and I have not the necessary equipment to do research myself, one would need Norman French, medieval Latin and the ability to read the scripts of the period but in the interest of general English history such an investigation ought to be made.

Events were happening in the world but we were unable to absorb them, it was the lichen-spotted pebble or the flat white shell that seemed important, not votes. Only two memories remain, but they are vivid ones, from those quiet, sleepy weeks. The first was hearing the Election results on the radio. We were not altogether surprised at Churchill's defeat, people who have been saved from some great danger often resent and hate their rescuers. The people were tired, he represented "blood, sweat and tears," yet without him we should have been a Nazi province with the population used as a source of slave labor. Changes were needed in England but they should have come after a period of reflection and rest, they should not have been plotted by a civil service largely out of touch with national feeling and pushed through Parliament in a hurry. Now and for a number of years the rule was to be "grab for yourself." Besides, our precipitate withdrawal from the East caused appalling suffering to peoples and races who had trusted us and has directly sowed the seeds of future wars. One of the worst experiences I ever had was when starving Pakistanis flung themselves on their knees in front of me a few years later, saying they were sorry they could bring me no gifts, but when would England come back and give them "British justice" again? I thought then and I think now that idealism is probably the greatest form of cruelty that exists unless it is sternly allied to common sense.

The other incident happened a few days later when we came back from the shore one morning to find Doris with a newspaper in her hand. A new type of bomb had exploded in Japan, thousands were dead, the war in the East was virtually over. Yet we were too tired for the atomic explosion to make much impression on us. Life had shrunk to one simple fact, was it war or peace in our own village? I have never been able to feel a particular fear of atomic weapons, it is as if the bombing in London had inoculated me against it. The people round me were saying that it would be far more merciful to go out with their families in a single moment than to face the dangers and separations of the last six years over again. The young protest because they have no idea of what our war was like. Yet without it they would not have their present freedom of expression. Sympathy and compassion are the luxuries of a long period of peace.

So we wandered back to the sands, they were our own again, the restrictions were relaxed and we were allowed to go fishing for a couple of hours. Our arguments were about the sugar ration, surely they would allow us more now that the blackberry crop was so big so that we could make some jam, or was the danger as great as they said about mines drifting in from the Atlantic and exploding on the shore? It was a world through which we moved as shadows, the rocks we touched seemed soft under the hot sun, yesterday was over although certain sights and sounds would always bring it back to us and our legacy was still the wartime saying, "Tomorrow never comes."

My conscience as a historian drove me back to London sooner than I need otherwise have gone but I wanted to see how people reacted to V-J Day, as Authority called Victory over Japan in the appalling bureaucratese they imposed on us. Turning everything into initials was surely a habit of the lower forms at school. Straight and picturesque slang was another matter because that could come directly from the heart. I was just in time to welcome Perdita, the Americans had flown her back from somewhere in Germany so that she could celebrate the ending of the war with her relatives and friends. If the English had thought of such a gesture, we agreed, they would have been ashamed of it. It might reveal emotion instead of indifference. So we collected a small Victory party at Lowndes; it included, among others, Norman Pearson, Gerald Henderson and Dean Lewens, the married daughter of my Cornish friend. She had been an army driver for most of the war. Hilda had remained in

Cornwall and Cole also was still in the country, waiting until the London apartment was properly repaired.

I felt at once something was wrong. I had dashed out earlier, notebook in hand, first for a long bus ride and then a walk but it was like an Old Folks Outing compared with Armistice Day, 1918. Then it had only been possible to stand with linked arms in what was usually a quiet street, while the populace yelled and stamped and screamed. I felt in my blood that we were going to pay heavily afterwards for the present imposed restraint. The Cockneys, I was told, and some of the foreign soldiers let themselves go later once they were drunk, otherwise it was the most dismal anticlimax that I have ever experienced. The Government did all in its power to damp down the spirits of the people and I am sure we have suffered from their folly ever since. It is true that there was a general feeling of shame; people knew by now that they had lost relatives, friends and possessions because of the policy of Appeasement but although the censorship could prevent any open expression of this in the newspapers it was the general opinion at this time of apparent victory. "They should never have let it happen" was the phrase most frequently heard.

Six people slept in our sitting room that night, most of them on the floor although one lucky individual got the sofa. I made no noble gesture, I stuck firmly to my own bed. The English covered themselves up with the flags that had been hanging out of their windows.

Life after V-J Day got slightly more difficult than before. The queues grew longer as people crowded back to London, the rations seemed smaller and the grumbling was much, much louder. I felt the power of the mob one morning when a naval officer tried to persuade us that there was no need to queue! We turned on him as one and he had to leave. We wanted to go into the shops and buy what we wanted without the constant handing over of dirty bits of paper. Frustration is the death of the spirit and no lion could have beaten our sulky roar.

At the end of October Robert invited me to Eckington for a brief holiday just as the leaves were beginning to turn. To celebrate, we took a train to York one day, our consciences at peace, it was a "necessary journey."

I had been once to York as a child but remembered little about it. I was particularly anxious to see the place again because of the delightful book that Margaret Phillips had written about her childhood there, *Within the City Wall.* I had written her immediately after reading it and we corresponded regularly, although we could not meet, until she came to Switzerland with her husband and two small children two years after the war. The first edition had to be a small one on account of the paper shortage but I cannot imagine why it has never been reprinted? I feel more and more as I discover such volumes by chance or through patient search that the publisher is often out of touch with what the public really enjoys and only looks for manuscripts that could be sold for film scripts. Yet the cinema and the library have different aims. I have been familiar with both and it is absurd to make either dependent on the other. There are times when people prefer to stay quietly in their own homes and they should not be deprived of a great deal of legitimate pleasure merely because a certain book does

172

not offer the typical movie situations. I have learned more about the evolution of the present age, its achievements and its dismal failures, from a number of records of childhood that I have collected, dating from about 1870 to the present time, than from serious historians. It is the crude material of our chronicle.

I had to report to Margaret that we could see little of the interior of the cathedral because it was still hidden under such limited protection as was possible in case it had been bombed. Still, they showed us the treasures in the crypt, among them was a horn covered with scenes said to have represented a festival of Mithra. The Wall was not so many marches north of York but there were many possibilities, a trader of any race could have brought it to the neighborhood, a Roman officer, the captain of a ship or a priest. It had survived the fierce battles of the Middle Ages and now the present war.

We were the first English sightseers, they told us, to come for several years although they had had a few American soldiers on leave. Afterwards, although it was late in the afternoon, we went and sat on a stone at a corner where we could look along the city walls.

It was cold, it was medieval rather than Saxon, yet as the darkness gathered I felt it almost as a hood clapped over my head and that I was hearing, rather than seeing, the tramp of a Saxon army with their axes. Stamford Bridge is not near York, it is much further north, but whereas most children remember Hastings, whoever thinks now of the great march south to Sussex after the great battle with the Northmen? Many of the soldiers must have had slight wounds, there were no proper roads, food must have been a difficulty. Naturally these thoughts got tangled up with our own "Battle for Britain." It had been a chance at Hastings, it had been a chance for us. How near we had been to a second conquest and to the probability that by the third generation all in England would be speaking German. We shivered as the sun went down, not only from cold, and as we walked back to the station in silence, both Robert and I were wondering by what design or lucky chance we had survived?

I went a last time to Renishaw. Next spring the rows of utility cabbages in the formal garden would give place to flowers. "I don't know how I should have got through without you, Bryher," Osbert said to my surprise as we wandered on across the fields. He had seemed a pillar of strength to us and how I could have been a help to him I could not imagine except that we had both been comrades in adversity. I had known instinctively how much he had missed Montegufoni and his "little Italian owls," just as he was the only one, really the only one, to understand that it was natural for me to think of Burier. I suppose few other of our friends could comprehend the divided feelings we shared; we were in England from a sense of duty and stuck it out because of "moral principles" rather than roots. It was a sad moment because I knew that I should never see Renishaw again in quite the same way. It was already drawing back into some private enchantment of its own while we were more aware than most of our friends of how much in the last years civilization had lost.

There are times when I do not care very much for the

human race. During the war when writers were considered "useless mouths," Osbert and Edith had fought to keep a skeleton of the arts alive. They gave parties to help the strays among us, they assisted those who were suffering not only from a lack of funds but extreme isolation, and although they did not agree with their views, they did their best to keep conscientious objectors from prison. A few intimate friends apart, nobody thanked them when the war was over. The people who owed them most laughed at them or attacked them, especially after they were safely dead. As for myself, I know I could not have endured those frightful years if it had not been for them and Hilda. They were too sensitive, most good writers are, but I think a later age will recognize them for what they were, Edith, a great poet, Osbert, a master of prose.

Osbert and I saw each other less frequently after the war but the deep bond from our common experiences endured until his death. The last time I saw him I tried to break through the reticence that had held both of us and tell him something of what he had meant to me during those terrible years. I think he understood. We knew it was a final meeting and before I was in Italy again, he died. I am glad that it was in the place he loved so much.

October 14th. The anniversary of the Battle of Hastings was on a Sunday this year and I went off in the afternoon for one of my City walks. To my astonishment I discovered a little steamer, it almost looked like a tug, preparing to leave with a dozen passengers for a half-hour trip along the Thames. I hurriedly joined it and although the water was dirty and the sky gray, I felt as if I were leaving for a Mediterranean cruise. My companions shared my enthusiasm, there were jokes about crossing the Channel and being gay in Paris while we ambled, if it is permissible to use such a word about a boat, almost to Southwark and then in a wide circle back to our starting point.

I had recently been studying a huge history of Southwark at the London Library, it would have needed a mule to carry it as far as Lowndes, and had discovered to my surprise that the Goodwins had owned most of the land there until the Conquest. It was rich farming country then so most of the widows and the children of the Saxon housecarls would have been dispossessed by the Norman men-at-arms. How near we had come, centuries later, to sharing their fate.

The boat trip stirred my blood, I wanted frantically to get away, people were collapsing all round me and I found myself standing in queues full of irritable people, thinking "How odd, how very odd, if I should crack." The feeling was one of complete frustration combined with anger over the Government's platitudes. "Why don't they do something to make life easier instead of talking so much?" was the comment I heard on every side. Of course it was difficult to reverse a national policy from war to peace but, a couple of years earlier, I should have chosen a small group that would have included psychological advisers, and asked them to work out a scheme to make the populace happier. It would have saved so much despair.

1946

This is a record of my war. It was a different one for each of us. I am sure we were not as afraid as people think, because towards the end most of us did not care whether we lived or died. It was partly the isolation. I often bumped against memories of Sylvia in my thoughts but I could not share my air-raid experiences with her nor she hers, of hardship and internment, with me. Our spasmodic Victory celebrations as I saw them were not rejoicings at all. (I believe it was different in Paris.) There was bad temper and disillusionment everywhere. The resentment of the last five years broke out in the queues where people shoved and grumbled instead of, as previously, keeping rigidly in line. The worst qualities of everyone, including myself, came not so much to the surface as shrieking out of us. The Londoners who had faced the Blitz were contemptuous of those who had gone into the country even if it had been by Government order. We accused them on their return of driving us out of our overcrowded buses and eating our food. Never believe the statement that a nation's character is purified by trial. It is simply not true.

Any ability that I had had to endure was due to two reasons. One was that I had foretold the conflict in 1932 and therefore had no guilt feelings. The other was my Freudian analysis with Dr. Hanns Sachs in the early Thirties. This helped me to put up with many privations because my energy was free to fight the enemy and from time to time the authorities; I did not have to fight my own mind. I can recommend the European type of analysis (it seems to have changed its direction in America) as the best antidote to bombing, frustration and hardship although one must not expect a miracle. What makes me angry is that we have the tools in our own hands to prevent a great deal of mass stupidity yet we seldom use them. Psychoanalysis is less for the neurotic than for the tough and healthy who can really use it to make the world a gayer and happier place in which to live. We should not ask too much from it; it cannot prevent the great oppositions of life where there are frequently several people involved, but it can answer some of the riddles of life and death and help us to understand our obstructions whether these are artificially imposed by the State or ones we invent ourselves. Once we know and comprehend our motives, we can often make the people round us happier. I have noticed that the people who have done the most good in their lives have usually had an unconventional education. We talk and talk, but I believe there is something profoundly wrong with the schools, license is as dangerous as repression, but in spite of some brave attempts we have done very little to work out a just and reasonable training for the young.

My desire now was to go and see Dr. Sachs again and tell him that if I had got through the war in tolerable shape it was due to our work together. He had settled in Boston in 1934 and I had seen him last in 1938. It was essential, however, for me to return to Switzerland first and he died almost the day that I landed in America. I have never known anyone else who had such an understanding of the mazes of the human mind.

It was a dismal winter of illness and collapse. The only rope that held us together was routine. Gradually the Lowndes Group began to disintegrate. Norman Pearson was the first to leave. He was recalled to America and we all missed his gaiety and Sunday visits. He had done so much to hold us together but what I admired myself was that he never whitewashed our difficulties nor held out hope of a return to a prewar world. I dislike people who "see the best in everything." It is easier to endure disasters when the facts are clear.

Perdita was next. She got permission to visit her

American relatives but as if the frustrations of the time wished to show that they still controlled our lives, we kept going to the airport only to be told that the flights had been canceled because of gales. She left eventually on February 23rd. We did not know although I think we suspected it that she would marry there, have a family and only return to Europe as a visitor.

Cole and Gerald went into the country for a time. It was natural for Cole to be unwilling to return to their only partially repaired apartment with its feeling of tragedy. The Sitwells retired for the winter to Renishaw. Molly Hughes, as gay and brave as ever, but visibly much older, came to spend the day with me. It was one of the last times I saw her because shortly afterwards she was obliged to leave the home she loved so much and go and live, first with her eldest son in Ireland and afterwards with the second one in South Africa where a few years later she died. I was very fond of her, she was so courageous but she became more and more bewildered and unhappy in a world from which the disciplines in which she firmly believed had gradually disappeared.

I lingered, partly because Hilda seemed ill and unwilling to make plans. She had had pneumonia badly during the First War and was so tall and thin that she had suffered more than most of us from the deficiencies of our rationing system. She shook her head when I spoke of Burier as if the effort of any travel was too much for her. Eventually some germ attacked her and she became seriously ill.

About this time my own permit arrived. It was only

valid for ten days and Hilda's doctor urged me to go out alone and find a clinic in Switzerland where she could be nursed back to health. He promised to provide the necessary certificates and get her out by air directly she was strong enough to travel. I was reluctant to leave her but I realized that it was the best thing to do. She reached Zurich early in May and lived there apart from long visits to the Tessin and America until her death in 1961.

I went a last time to Aldermanbury. It seemed to me that the heart of London, the soul of its resistance, was in the parish where Shakespeare and his fellowship of the Globe had lived, written and worked. Memory! Sometimes I ask myself what it is? I once knew a great deal about the Elizabethan age and heard its language ringing in my ears. Now it is a garden in the middle of the dust, faint, imprecise in outline, some passionate remembering out of focus of what was once there. I am thankful that I did not know that afternoon that St. Mary's, where Heminge was a churchwarden and where, with Condell, he saved the Folio for us, was soon to be taken down stone by stone and sent to America. At first, when I heard that news, I could not believe it. Afterwards I thought, let it be. America will preserve what we discard. If our past, our poetry, our greatness, has no longer any meaning for us, why cling to an empty symbol; let it go, still rich and living, to another land. But on that March day there were daisies, even a tiny daffodil, growing out of the stones.

April 1st. Hilda was asleep and they asked me not to wake her in case she should be upset. I stole out although it seemed wrong to leave almost secretly after we had shared five years and a half of the Blitz and its hardships together. I went out to the airport near Croydon from which I had made my first flight in 1924. Then it had been only to Paris and it had taken several hours. It seemed as if again I were going back to my beginnings. I remember pushing through various controls in what was apparently a vast hangar, but nothing of the journey until we landed at Geneva.

The passport officer recognized me and smiled. I was handed a Swiss ration book. A passenger, also from the plane, pointed in awe at a shop window. "Bananas!" he said. "They've got bananas." None had been seen in England since 1940. The heating plant at Burier had collapsed soon after I had left so I was going to stay with Elsie. She owned a little house at Pully near Lausanne. Luckily I got a train almost at once.

The dogs barked and wagged their tails but as I had expected, they did not recognize me. Elsie and I hugged each other. Everything was familiar yet totally strange. "I'm back," I said, an obvious remark with Claudi sniffing hopefully at my pockets for a biscuit and Elsie answered, hugging me again, "Yes, you're home."

Index